A SPEECH IMPROVEMENT DRILLBOOK

The Sounds of American English

Thomas D. Houchin
St. John's University, New York

AMSCO COLLEGE PUBLICATIONS
315 Hudson Street   New York, N.Y. 10013

ISBN 0-87720-974-X
Specify CR 181 P or THE SOUNDS OF AMERICAN ENGLISH

Published in 1976 by Amsco College Publications, a division
of Amsco School Publications, Inc.

Printed in the United States of America

Preface

This book contains a series of twenty lessons which provides the opportunity for instruction in the sounds that may make a difference in meaning in American English. It is intended for basic college speech classes, and may also be used by teachers of English as a second language.

The lessons are based upon a form of "General American" speech. Most experts in phonetics accept at least three major speech regions of American English, namely, Eastern, Southern, and General American. Definite boundaries for American speech regions are less easily drawn than for those of many foreign languages. There are, of course, at least a dozen regional variations of American English and many more variations of *them*. The author chose for this book the General American speech standard used by most network radio and television broadcasters. It is their speech which is difficult to assign to any one speech region, and which cuts across most educational and economic levels in the United States today. There are, however, some references to other speech regions of American English within the lessons themselves.

The materials for practice are colloquial, and are free from tongue-twisters and childish phrases. They contain a number of words which are mispronounced in the major speech regions of the United States. Because of the conversational nature of the practice sentences, there is hope that improved speech will transfer from the classroom to the student's everyday life.

Because of the lack of correspondence between English spelling and pronunciation, the International Phonetic Alphabet

(IPA) is used to refer to the sounds. Teachers will discover that students readily adapt to the symbols. For those teachers and students who prefer the dictionary diacritical marks, there is the system of *Webster's New Collegiate Dictionary*, published by the G. & C. Merriam Company, printed immediately below the phonetic symbol for each lesson. A useful supplement to a college-level dictionary is the Merriam publication by John S. Kenyon and Thomas A. Knott, *A Pronouncing Dictionary of American English*, which lists in the same phonetic system adopted in this book most of the words used by educated speakers.

The lessons follow the order of those English sounds often needed for speech improvement practice. The less common sounds of English are treated generally in the later lessons. The author has placed sounds with similar characteristics, such as the nasal sounds, and other sounds with similar production, in the same lesson. The result is, thus, an order of lessons based upon teaching experience. In order to make each lesson a complete unit in itself, there is some repetition of the requirements for effective voice production and pronunciation.

The word lists contain the sound of the lesson first in the initial position, then the sound in the middle of the word, and finally the sound at the end of the word. Each of the sounds of English, however, does not occur in all positions. This will account, for example, for the fact that the sound of *i* as in *in* does not occur at the end of words. In addition, the *ng* sound of s*ing* and the sound of *z* in a*z*ure do not ordinarily occur at the beginning of words.

All of the words, pairs of words, and sentences are numbered. The numbers are important in order to identify any material for later review and practice by the teacher and the student.

The selections of poetry and prose are a necessary part of any program of speech improvement. They are to be read aloud in class by students, with the instructor emphasizing appropriate corrections with specific reference to the sound of the lesson.

By means of the materials of this book, it is possible to locate and remedy students' specific speech improvement needs, and to plan a program for further improvement.

The author wishes to acknowledge the contributions of Professors Ken Fountain and Betty Tucker Ferguson, of the Speech Department, Miami-Dade Community College–North, and Dr. LeRoy Pavés, who have read the manuscript and made helpful suggestions.

Contents

Acknowledgments

Grateful acknowledgment is made to the following sources for permission to use copyrighted materials appearing in this book.

Norma Millay Ellis. "Recuerdo," from *Collected Poems*, Harper & Row, copyright 1922, 1950 by Edna St. Vincent Millay and Norma Millay Ellis.

Harcourt Brace Jovanovich, Inc. "Prelude I," from *Collected Poems 1909–1962*, copyright 1936, © 1963, 1964 by T. S. Eliot. "The Watcher," from *In an Iridescent Time*, copyright © 1957 by Ruth Stone; originally published in *The New Yorker*.

Holt, Rinehart and Winston, Inc. "The Road Not Taken," "Fire and Ice," and "Mowing," from *The Poetry of Robert Frost*, edited by Edward Connery Lathem, copyright 1916, 1934, 1944, 1951, © 1962, 1969 by Robert Frost.

Little, Brown and Company. "So Run Along and Play," from *Take Sky*, copyright © 1961, 1962 by David McCord. "The Starry Night," from *White Paper*, copyright © 1963 by George Starbuck; originally published in *The New Yorker*.

Macmillan Publishing Co., Inc. "Factory Windows Are Always Broken," from *Collected Poems*, copyright 1914 by Vachel Lindsay, renewed 1942 by Elizabeth C. Lindsay.

Ellen C. Masters. "Lucinda Matlock," from *Spoon River Anthology*, Macmillan, copyright 1914, 1915, 1916, 1942, 1944 by Edgar Lee Masters.

New Directions Publishing Corp. "Do Not Go Gentle Into That Good Night," from *The Poems of Dylan Thomas*, copyright 1952 by Dylan Thomas. "Peter's Little Daughter Dies," from *Collected Poems*, copyright 1939 by Kenneth Patchen.

Helen Thurber. "The Bear Who Let It Alone" and "The Rabbits Who Caused All the Trouble," from *Fables for Our Time*, Harper & Row, copyright 1940 by James Thurber, copyright © 1968 by Helen Thurber; originally published in *The New Yorker*. From "The Night the Ghost Got In," from *My Life and Hard Times*, Harper & Row, copyright 1933, © 1961 by James Thurber; originally published in *The New Yorker*.

The Viking Press, Inc. "Girl's-Eye View of Relatives: First Lesson," from *Times Three*, copyright © 1959 by Phyllis McGinley; originally published in *The New Yorker*.

Wesleyan University Press. "The Missing Person," from *Night Light*, copyright © 1966 by Donald Justice; originally published in *The New Yorker*.

Notes to the Student

Throughout the lessons, the sounds will be referred to as "voiceless" or "voiced." Your teacher will often ask you to check this aspect of speech by putting your hand securely against your larynx, which is commonly called the "Adam's apple," while you produce the sound. By this means you will be able to feel the slight vibration of the larynx itself, which is caused by the movement of the vocal cords or folds within the larynx for each voiced sound.

All vowels and all diphthongs are voiced. The three nasal sounds are voiced. The sounds /l/, /r/, /w/, and /j/ (as in *l*ook, *r*ug, *w*ave, and *y*ard) are voiced. /h/ (as in *h*at) is voiceless. /hw/ (as in *wh*eel) begins with a voiceless sound but rapidly adds a voiced element.

The remaining consonants are listed below in so-called cognate pairs—that is, pairs that are produced in the same manner except that one is voiceless and the other is voiced.

Voiceless	*Voiced*
/ t / as in *t*ale	/ d / as in *d*ime
/ θ / as in *th*ank	/ ð / as in *th*at
/ s / as in *s*ing	/ z / as in *z*ero
/ k / as in *k*itten	/ g / as in *g*arden
/ f / as in *f*ace	/ v / as in *v*ery
/ p / as in *p*a*p*er	/ b / as in *b*ack
/ ʃ / as in *sh*e	/ ʒ / as in a*z*ure
/ tʃ / as in *ch*air	/ dʒ / as in *j*ust

The International Phonetic Alphabet, which is used to symbolize the English sounds in this book, has come from a variety of sources. The voiceless *th* sound has a symbol, /θ/, from Greek; the symbol for the voiced *th* sound, /ð/, comes from Old English. The sound value of the *y* as in *year* has the symbol /j/, which is the pronunciation of the letter *j* in German and in the Scandinavian languages. It is most important for you to remember that the *same symbol* is always used for the *same sound*, regardless of the letters used to spell the word.

If you would also like to use any of the words of the lessons to improve your vocabulary, it will be helpful to use small cards on one side of which you write a word and on the reverse side the definition of the word. If your native language is not English, you may write the English word on one side with the translation in your native language on the reverse side. Cards such as these will help you learn a great number of words in a short time by means of frequent periods of drill.

You may find a mirror helpful in following both the drawing of the mouth position and the specific explanation of the production of each sound. On page 5 you will find a chart of the organs and structures used in the sounds of American English. At several points in the lessons you may want to refer again to the chart as you study certain sounds.

Your dictionary will help you to add to the lists of words in the exercises whenever you need additional practice for mastery of a sound or whenever you need special words for educational, business, or professional use. In the lists, any word with the same pronunciation as the example but with a different meaning and spelling is given between parentheses after the listed word.

There are, in addition, word and sentence drills which contrast the sounds of the lessons with other sounds that may cause confusion or difficulty. These exercises serve a number of purposes, including increased familiarity with the sound of the lesson, improved auditory discrimination of the sounds of English, and increased vocabulary.

Concerning the selections of poetry and prose, if you find one of the readings of special interest, you may find other selections by the same author in almost any library. You may, of course, use your own favorite selections of poetry and prose for oral reading and practice. For all of your practice with the selections of poetry and prose, you and your teacher should first discuss the sound or sounds on which you will concentrate.

The amount of time needed for each lesson depends upon the practice you require to master any given sound. The lessons in this book are designed for speech improvement and are not, of course, a substitute for speech therapy.

Mastery of spoken English is not easy; however, the materials in this book are of proven value for gaining an oral command of our language.

The Organs and the Structures Used in the Sounds of American English

1. Lips
2. Teeth
3. Upper gum ridge
4. Hard palate
5. Soft palate
6. Uvula, which should be relaxed for the nasal sounds and relatively raised for all other sounds
7. Nasal passage
8. Mouth, or oral cavity
9. Tongue
10. Tip of tongue
11. Middle of tongue
12. Back of tongue
13. Pharynx, the space in the throat
14. Epiglottis, the covering of the larynx
15. Larynx, commonly called the "Adam's apple"
16. Vocal cords, which may also be called folds, and glottis, the space between the vocal cords for air to pass, whether or not it is vibrated by the vocal cords at various pitch levels
17. Trachea, or wind pipe, the passageway for air to and from the lungs
18. Esophagus, or gullet, the passageway for liquid and food to the stomach

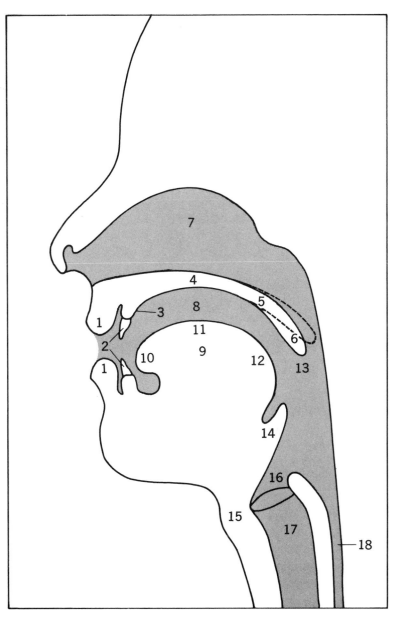

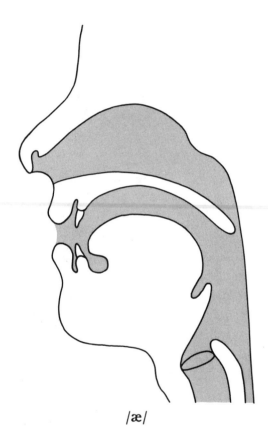

/æ/

LESSON 1

/æ/ as in *add*
(*Dictionary mark:* a)

To make the vowel /æ/, your mouth should be somewhat open, the lips slightly spread and relaxed, and the tongue should be low enough so that it does not touch your upper molars. Also, the tongue should have a concave shape with an arch in the back.

Always voice the /æ/ sound fully with a relaxed throat. To make sure you are voicing this sound, put your hand securely against your larynx, the "Adam's apple," in order to feel its slight vibration as you produce this sound.

Perhaps you will be able to say the /æ/ sound in "had," "have," and "happy" but fail in words such as "ham," "hand," and "hang." The reason you may mispronounce the last three words is that they contain nasal sounds, /m/, /n/, and /ŋ/, which should come through your nose. The /æ/ sound should not be nasalized.

Keep these questions in mind during your practice. Is your mouth somewhat open? Is your tongue down in front so that it does not touch your upper molars? Does the air stream come through your mouth rather than your nose?

Remember to keep your mouth open, the /æ/ sound short, and the air stream directed well forward—that is, out of the mouth, not through the nose.

I. /æ/ Words

Listen to your instructor pronounce these words. Repeat them aloud in class and practice them afterward.

1. absolute	11. Anne	21. band	31. hang
2. act	12. antagonistic	22. candle	32. happy
3. action	13. apple	23. can't	33. hat
4. Adam	14. ashes	24. cash (cache)	34. have
5. add	15. ask	25. catch	35. landing
6. after	16. atom	26. clam	36. mat
7. alley	17. attitude	27. clash	37. path
8. ample	18. aunt (ant)	28. had	38. sang
9. anchor	19. avenue	29. ham	39. than
10. animal	20. average	30. hand	40. that

II. Contrasting Pairs

Your instructor will pronounce the following pairs of words and the sentences for you to repeat aloud in class and practice when you are alone. Note that the word containing the sound of this lesson is italicized.

1. shell — *shall*
   Shell the beans.
   Shall we go?
2. pet — *pat*
   Did you pet your dog?
   Did you pat your cushion?
3. pen — *pan*
   The pen won't break.
   The pan won't break.
4. set — *sat*
   He set the glass on that table.
   He sat on the new chair.

5. head — *had*
   Let's head for the shower.
   He's had a fine experience.
6. beg — *bag*
   Does your dog beg?
   May I carry your bag?
7. kin — *can*
   Are you next of kin?
   Are you sure you can?
8. bet — *bat*
   You can bet on that one!
   Will you bat the ball?
9. bed — *bad*
   That's an antique bed.
   That's just too bad.
10. luck — *lack*
    Good luck with your exams.
    You lack fifty cents.

III. /æ/ Words and Sentences

The following words and sentences provide additional practice for you on the sound of this lesson.

1. action
   There was a lot of action on the football field Friday.
2. add
   Please add the column correctly.
3. atom, has
   Modern research on the atom has aided medical science.
4. animal
   I enjoyed the play *The Male Animal*.
5. Anne
   Anne is my best friend.

6. class

   He was on a Class A baseball team.
7. Saturday

   My vacation begins a week from Saturday.
8. catch

   Did the police catch the driver?
9. back

   When did you get back from your trip?
10. ran, dash

    He ran the 200-yard dash in record time.
11. handkerchief

    The handkerchief was important in the play.
12. damp

    It was a damp morning.

IV. Poetry

Listen as your instructor reads these two poems aloud. Follow along and note that all occurrences of the /æ/ sound are emphasized. You may have an opportunity to read a portion of the poems in class; practice this reading by yourself as well.

Meeting at Night

The gray sea and the long black land;
And the yellow half-moon large and low;
And the startled little waves that leap
In fiery ringlets from their sleep,
As I gain the cove with pushing prow,
And quench its speed in the slushy sand.

Then a mile of warm sea-scented beach;
Three fields to cross till a farm appears;
A tap at the pane, the quick sharp scratch

a bird

And blue spurt of a lighted match,
And a voice less loud, through its joys and fears,
Than the two hearts beating each to each!

—Robert Browning

Factory Windows Are Always Broken

Factory windows are always broken.
Somebody's always throwing bricks,
Somebody's always heaving cinders,
Playing ugly Yahoo tricks.

Factory windows are always broken.
Other windows are let alone.
No one throws through the chapel-window
The bitter, snarling, derisive stone.

Factory windows are always broken.
Something or other is going wrong.
Something is rotten—I think, in Denmark.
End of the factory-window song.

—Vachel Lindsay

LESSON 2

/aʊ/ as in *out*
(*Dictionary mark:* aủ)

/aʊ/ is a diphthong, which means one vowel sound gliding into another in the same syllable—in this case, /a/ and /ʊ/. To begin this sound, your mouth should be well open and your tongue should rest on the floor of your mouth. Think of these two sounds as one sound and keep /aʊ/ short. To complete this diphthong, begin raising your tongue as you begin rounding your lips.

Voice /aʊ/ fully so that you can be easily heard. To make sure you are voicing this sound, put your hand securely against your larynx in order to feel its slight vibration as you produce this diphthong.

You will be successful if you begin /aʊ/ with your mouth well open and your tongue on the floor of your mouth, and if you complete the diphthong quickly.

I. /aʊ/ Words

Listen to your instructor pronounce these words. Repeat them aloud in class and practice them afterward.

1. hourglass	3. our (hour)	5. out	7. outlaw
2. ounce	4. oust	6. outcome	8. outrageous

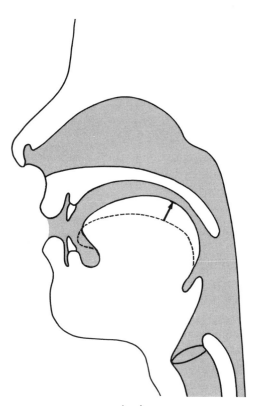

/aʊ/

9. ourselves	18. doubt	26. round	34. cow
10. owl	19. down	27. shout	35. endow
11. about	20. flower	28. sound	36. how
12. around	(flour)	29. town	37. now
13. brown	21. found	30. vowel	38. plow
14. clown	22. growl	31. allow	39. prow
15. couch	23. house	32. bough	40. vow
16. count	24. loud	(bow)	
17. devour	25. power	33. brow	

The following words contain nasal sounds, /m/, /n/, and

/ŋ/, preceding the /aʊ/ sound. The nasal sounds should not cause you to nasalize /aʊ/ as well.

1. mouth   2. noun   3. bring out   4. running out

II. Contrasting Pairs

Your instructor will pronounce the following pairs of words and the sentences for you to repeat aloud in class and practice when you are alone. Note that the word containing the sound of this lesson is italicized.

1. shut – *shout*
   Always shut the attic door.
   Never shout that loud again.
2. hull – *howl*
   The hull of the boat needs painting.
   The howl of the wind warned us.
3. but – *bout*
   We will help, but not without you.
   A bout with pneumonia exhausted him.
4. shot – *shout*
   The shot faded away.
   The shout faded away.
5. spotted – *spouted*
   Rain spotted his coat.
   Rain spouted from the gutter.
6. none – *noun*
   None of these will do.
   Every one of her poems begins with a noun.
7. Dan – *down*
   Dan ran through the fog.
   He was down before he knew it.
8. mass – *mouse*
   What a mass of clouds!
   What a large mouse!

9. tan – *town*
   Wear the tan coat.
   Union is a small town.
10. lad – *loud*
    He's a mere lad.
    He's a bit loud.

III. /aʊ/ Words and Sentences

The following words and sentences provide additional practice for you on the sound of this lesson.

1. hour
   An hour seems short when you are busy.
2. our
   It was our plan to finish the job.
3. ounce
   The scales weighed every ounce correctly.
4. count
   The child was just learning to count.
5. around
   She walked around the campus on Sunday afternoon.
6. brown
   I like the brown suit better than the blue one.
7. how
   She didn't know how to ship the boxes.
8. oust
   Some of the club members tried to oust the president.
9. bough
   The wind broke the bough of the tree.
10. out
    He looked out the window at the rain.
11. now
    It seems that now is the best time.

12. outline

   Haven't you written your outline yet?

13. down

   Do you think the pen you lost is down there?

14. thou

   The word "thou" is not commonly used today.

15. endow

   We hope he will endow the project.

16. mouse

   The dog tried to catch the mouse.

17. about

   What do you know about that subject?

18. allow

   I don't think his adviser will allow him to do it.

19. running out

   The examination period was running out.

IV. Poetry

Listen as your instructor reads this poem aloud. Follow along and underline each occurrence of the /aʊ/ sound. You may have an opportunity to read a portion of the poem in class; practice this reading by yourself as well.

Mowing

There was never a sound beside the wood but one,
And that was my long scythe whispering to the ground.
What was it it whispered? I knew not well myself;
Perhaps it was something about the heat of the sun,
Something, perhaps, about the lack of sound—
And that was why it whispered and did not speak.
It was no dream of the gift of idle hours,
Or easy gold at the hand of fay or elf:

Anything more than the truth would have seemed too weak
To the earnest love that laid the swale in rows,
Not without feeble pointed spikes of flowers
(Pale orchises), and scared a bright green snake.
The fact is the sweetest dream that labor knows.
My long scythe whispered and left the hay to make.

—Robert Frost

Did you underline these words in the poem? Sound, ground, about, sound, hours, without, flowers.

LESSON 3

/aɪ/ as in *icing*
(*Dictionary mark:* ī)

To make the /aɪ/ sound, your mouth should be well open for the first sound of this diphthong, which means two vowels in one syllable—in this case, /a/ and /ɪ/. To complete this diphthong, begin raising your tongue as you slightly retract your lips and move your jaw upward. Voice /aɪ/ fully so that you can be easily heard.

Keep these questions in mind during your practice: Do you open your mouth wide for the initial /a/? Does your jaw move vertically upward when gliding to the second element?

I. /aɪ/ Words

Listen to your instructor pronounce these words. Repeat them aloud in class and practice them afterward.

1. aisle (I'll)	7. Irish	13. cried
2. eye (I)	8. iron	14. dive
3. icing	9. isolation	15. fine
4. idea	10. item	16. fire
5. identify	11. itinerary	17. five
6. idle	12. ivory	18. might

19. mind	25. by (buy, bye)	31. my
20. mine	26. defy	32. pie
21. pile	27. die (dye)	33. rye
22. time	28. guy	34. shy
23. tire	29. high	35. sigh
24. wide	30. lie (lye)	36. tie

II. Contrasting Pairs

Your instructor will pronounce the following pairs of words and sentences for you to repeat aloud in class and practice when

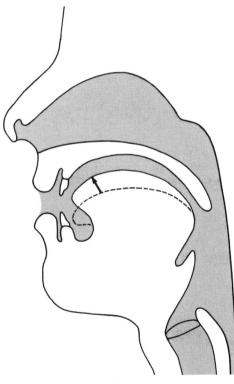

/aɪ/

you are alone. Note that the word containing the sound of this lesson is italicized.

1. oil – *aisle*
   Jerry slipped in the oil.
   Jerry slipped in the aisle.
2. down – *dine*
   Down your breakfast!
   Dine with us at eight!
3. pup – *pipe*
   It was only a small pup.
   It was only a small pipe.
4. point – *pint*
   That's the point of our discussion.
   That's a pint of milk.
5. top – *type*
   Can you top that?
   Can you type that?
6. noun – *nine*
   Where's the noun in your sentence?
   It's half past nine.
7. boy – *buy*
   It belongs to a little boy.
   It depends on what you buy.
8. fun – *fine*
   It's fun!
   It's fine!
9. bout – *bite*
   She had a bout with measles.
   Take a big bite.
10. mouse – *mice*
    A mouse nestled there.
    Some mice nestled there.

III. /aɪ/ Words and Sentences

The following words and sentences provide additional practice for you on the sound of this lesson.

1. aisle
   He walked down the center aisle at the church.
2. I
   It was strange that I hadn't noticed it before.
3. find
   Were you able to find out when the train leaves?
4. five
   He was planning to spend five weeks in Canada.
5. skywriting
   They watched the skywriting.
6. idea
   Didn't the idea seem good to you?
7. island
   The island was a popular resort.
8. white, tie
   He was given a blue and white tie for Christmas.
9. I, pie
   I prefer pie to cake.
10. mile
    Do you want to walk one mile or two?
11. buy
    When are you going to buy the tickets?
12. bye
    "Good-bye," they shouted as we left their home.
13. shine
    You can almost see yourself in the shine of his shoes.
14. item
    He had several good reasons for each item he wanted to purchase.

15. kind

The professor was very kind.

16. light

The light shone through my bedroom window.

17. die

The grass was about to die from lack of water.

18. eyes

Her eyes were dark brown.

19. mile, high

Denver is called the "Mile-High City."

IV. Poetry

Listen as your instructor reads this poem aloud. Follow along and underline each occurrence of the /aɪ/ sound. You may have an opportunity to read a portion of the poem in class; practice this reading by yourself as well.

Fire and Ice

Some say the world will end in fire,
Some say in ice.
From what I've tasted of desire
I hold with those who favor fire.
But if it had to perish twice,
I think I know enough of hate
To say that for destruction ice
Is also great
And would suffice.

—Robert Frost

Did you underline these words in the poem? Fire, ice, I've, desire, I, fire, twice, I, I, ice, suffice.

LESSON 4

/ɛ/ as in penny
(*Dictionary mark:* e)

For the sound of this lesson your tongue is relaxed, relatively low in your mouth, and your lips are slightly drawn back. Try to make the /ɛ/ sound short. Remember to keep the air stream through your mouth, using a full voice.

I. /ɛ/ Words

Listen to your instructor pronounce these words. Repeat them aloud in class and practice them afterward.

1. any	13. against	25. pen
2. edit	14. beg	26. pencil
3. edge	15. cent (scent)	27. penny
4. eggs	16. chair	28. pleasure
5. elm	17. defect	29. professional
6. else	18. get	30. sense
7. engine	19. guess	31. seven
8. entertain	20. lemon	32. spent
9. entry	21. measure	33. ten
10. every	22. men	34. treasure
11. excellent	23. met	35. twenty
12. extra	24. parents	36. very

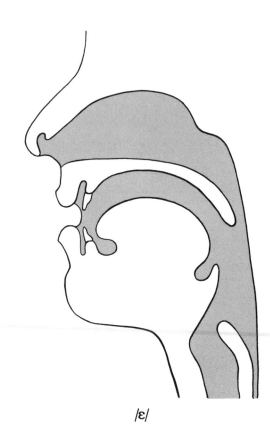

/ɛ/

II. Contrasting Pairs

Your instructor will pronounce the following pairs of words and
the sentences for you to repeat aloud in class and practice when
you are alone. Note that the word containing the sound of this
lesson is italicized.

  1. sail – *sell*
     She is mending the sail.
     That won't sell.

2. bait – *bet*
   I'll bait your hook.
   I'll bet you a dollar.
3. fail – *fell*
   It can't fail.
   It almost fell.
4. pup – *pep*
   Where did you get your pup?
   Where did you get your pep?
5. pat – *pet*
   She gave her hair-do one last pat.
   If you pet the dog, it won't bark.
6. bill – *bell*
   Tomorrow is the tax bill hearing.
   One bell means dismissal.
7. pin – *pen*
   My pin is broken!
   My pen is broken!
8. shall – *shell*
   Shall we go now?
   Shell the beans quickly!
9. late – *let*
   Late again?
   Let us alone.
10. laid – *lead*
    He laid it there two weeks ago.
    It's lead, not iron.

III. /ɛ/ Words and Sentences

The following words and sentences provide additional practice for you on the sound of this lesson.

1. any, when
   He didn't have any money when he returned from town.

2. edge
   We looked over the edge of the cliff.
3. egg, breakfast
   I fried an egg and toasted some bread for breakfast.
4. Fred, left, end
   The coach chose Fred for the left end.
5. enter
   They hoped to enter the university this fall.
6. any, extra
   The paper boy did not have any extra newspapers.
7. bed, very
   The dormitory bed was not very soft.
8. get, help, project
   Was he able to get some help with his project?
9. help, chest
   "Help your neighbor" was the slogan for the Community Chest.
10. met, friends, several
    We met some friends we had not seen for several years.
11. pen, well, anymore
    My pen does not hold ink well anymore.
12. them, directions
    She asked them the directions to the campus.

IV. Prose

Listen as your instructor reads this story aloud. Follow along and note that all occurrences of the /ɛ/ sound are emphasized. You may have the opportunity to read a portion of the story in class; practice this reading by yourself as well.

The Bear Who Let It Alone

In the woods of the Far West there once lived a brown bear who could take it or let it alone. He would go into a bar where they sold mead, a fermented drink made of honey, and he would have just two drinks. Then he would put some money on the bar and say, "See what the bears in the back room will have," and he would go home. But finally he took to drinking by himself most of the day. He would reel home at night, kick over the umbrella stand, knock down the bridge lamps, and ram his elbows through the windows. Then he would collapse on the floor and lie there until he went to sleep. His wife was greatly distressed and his children were very frightened.

At length the bear saw the error of his ways and began to reform. In the end he became a famous teetotaller and a persistent temperance lecturer. He would tell everybody that came to his house about the awful effects of drink, and he would boast about how strong and well he had become since he gave up touching the stuff. To demonstrate this, he would stand on his head and on his hands and he would turn cartwheels in the house, kicking over the umbrella stand, knocking down the bridge lamps, and ramming his elbows through the windows. Then he would lie down on the floor, tired by his healthful exercise, and go to sleep. His wife was greatly distressed and his children were very frightened.

Moral: You might as well fall flat on your face as lean over too far backward.

—James Thurber

LESSON 5

/t/, /d/ as in *t*ale and *d*ime
(*Dictionary marks:* t, d)

To make /t/ and /d/, put the tip of your tongue just above your upper front teeth; the sound is then produced as the tip of the tongue is quickly retracted. /t/ and /d/ sometimes have a small "puff" of air immediately after their correct pronunciation.

/t/ and /d/ are formed in the same way, but /t/ is voiceless while /d/ is voiced in the larynx. It is difficult to feel the slight vibration of the larynx as you produce the /d/ sound because of its short duration.

I. /t/ and /d/ Words

Listen to your instructor pronounce these words. Repeat them aloud in class and practice them afterward.

1. tale (tail)	7. auto	13. fate
2. tame	8. potato	14. fight
3. told	9. sister	15. out
4. dime	10. hidden	16. hood
5. doom	11. sudden	17. loud
6. door	12. window	18. sold

These words are sometimes incorrectly pronounced. Be sure

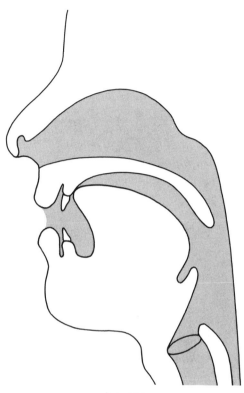

/t/, /d/

to sound the /t/ or /d/ in the middle of the words.

1. bottle	3. little	5. couldn't	7. shouldn't
2. bottom	4. metal	6. didn't	8. wouldn't

When you pronounce these words, be sure to sound the final /t/ or /d/.

1. about	4. left	7. band	10. land
2. count	5. must	8. gold	11. old
3. ghost	6. west	9. good	12. rid

Be careful not to substitute the /d/ for the correct /t/ sound in these words.

1. liberty	5. thirty	9. city
2. equality	6. forty	10. matter
3. fraternity	7. fifty	11. bitter
4. twenty	8. mighty	12. waiting

II. Contrasting Pairs

Your instructor will pronounce the following pairs of words for you to repeat aloud in class. Practice them when you are alone.

| 1. ant – and | 3. built – build | 5. rate – raid |
| 2. bent – bend | 4. colt – cold | 6. site – side |

All of the following words end in *ed*, but the endings in the first column are pronounced /t/ while the endings in the second column are pronounced /d/.

Since the /k/ in "liked" is a voiceless sound, voiceless /t/ must follow. Since the /g/ in "lagged" is voiced, voiced /d/ must follow.

| 1. liked – lagged | 3. ripped – razzed |
| 2. passed – prowled | 4. talked – tied |

In the following words, the *ed* ending is a separate syllable, following *t* or *d*. In such words, the *ed* is always pronounced /ɪd/—the /ɪ/ sound will be discussed in Lesson 12.

| 1. counted | 3. pointed |
| 2. needed | 4. wanted |

III. /t/ and /d/ Words and Sentences

The following words and sentences provide additional practice for you on the sounds of this lesson.

1. table, set
   The table was set for five people.

2. due, today
My paper is due one week from today.
3. student, wanted, to, travel
The student wanted to travel in the spring.
4. day
The day began cool and clear.
5. child, preferred, drops
The child preferred gum drops.
6. deep
The river is deep here.
7. bread
I like the smell of fresh bread.
8. to, do, better, second, test
He was able to do better on the second test.
9. about, thirty
She was about thirty years old.
10. it, to, withdraw, fifty, dollars, trip
It will be necessary to withdraw fifty dollars for your trip.
11. turn, light
Turn on the light.
12. did, last
Did you see the play last week?

IV. Poetry

Listen as your instructor reads this poem aloud. Follow along and note that all occurrences of the /t/ and /d/ sounds are emphasized. You may have an opportunity to read a portion of the poem in class; practice this reading by yourself as well.

Recuerdo

We were very *tired*, we were very merry—
We had gone back and forth all night on the ferry.
It was bare and bright, and smelled like a stable—
But we looked into a fire, we leaned across a table,
We lay on a hill-top underneath the moon;
And the whistles kept blowing, and the dawn came soon.

We were very *tired*, we were very merry—
We had gone back and forth all night on the ferry;
And you ate an apple, and I ate a pear,
From a dozen of each we had bought somewhere;
And the sky went wan, and the wind came cold,
And the sun rose dripping, a bucketful of gold.

We were very *tired*, we were very merry,
We had gone back and forth all night on the ferry.
We hailed, "Good morrow, mother!" to a shawl-covered head,
And bought a morning paper, which neither of us read;
And she wept, "God bless you!" for the apples and pears,
And we gave her all our money but our subway fares.

—Edna St. Vincent Millay

LESSON 6

/ θ /, / ð / as in *th*ank and *th*at
(*Dictionary marks:* th, <u>th</u>)

You should make the *th* sounds with your tongue slightly between your teeth.

There are two *th* sounds, the voiceless /θ/ as in "thank," and the voiced /ð/ as in "that." To make sure you are voicing the sound as in the word "that," put your hand securely against your larynx in order to feel its slight vibration as you produce the sound.

Repeat both of the key words of this lesson, prolonging /θ/ and /ð/.

I. /θ/ and /ð/ Words

Listen to your instructor pronounce these words. Repeat them aloud in class and practice them afterward.

1. birthday – leather
2. booth – soothe
3. breath – breathe
4. something – another
5. thank – that
6. thought – though

II. Contrasting Pairs

Your instructor will pronounce the following pairs of words for

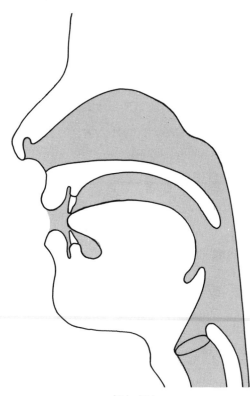

/θ/, /ð/

you to repeat aloud in class and practice when you are alone.

/θ/ - /t/

1. both   – boat
2. death   – debt
3. faithful – fateful
4. thank   – tank
5. thought – taught
6. three   – tree

/ð/ - /d/

1. breathe – breed
2. loathe   – load
3. other   – udder
4. then   – den
5. there   – dare
6. they   – day

/θ/ – /f/

1. death	– deaf		3. thread	– Fred
2. thin	– fin		4. three	– free

/ð/ – /v/

1. than	– van		3. they'll	– veil
2. that	– vat		4. thou	– vow

III. /θ/ and /ð/ Words and Sentences

The following words and sentences provide additional practice for you on the sounds of this lesson.

1. author : /θ/
   Shakespeare was his favorite author.
2. the, theory : /ð/, /θ/
   The scientist had a revolutionary theory.
3. the, thing : /ð/, /θ/
   His point of view was the most important thing.
4. thought, the, the : /θ/, /ð/, /ð/
   She thought about the solution to the problem.
5. the, faithful : /ð/, /θ/
   The dog was faithful to his master.
6. something, the : /θ/, /ð/
   Something caused the car to stop.
7. breath, weather : /θ/, /ð/
   You can see your breath in cold weather.
8. the, bath, there : /ð/, /θ/, /ð/
   The shower and bath facilities were good there.
9. thought, the, north : /θ/, /ð/, /θ/
   I thought the building faced north.
10. them : /ð/
    We saw them downtown today.
11. rather, than : /ð/, /ð/
    Would you rather go to Washington than Philadelphia?

12. these, they : /ð/, /ð/
    These gloves look as if they would be warm.
13. another : /ð/
    He asked for another glass of milk.
14. either : /ð/
    You may either write a paper or make a speech.
15. the, weather, this : /ð/, /ð/, /ð/
    The weather is not so hot this summer as last.
16. the, mother, bathe, the : /ð/, /ð/, /ð/, /ð/
    The mother had to bathe the baby every day.
17. breathe, the : /ð/, /ð/
    It was difficult to breathe in the smoky room.

IV. Prose

Listen as your instructor reads this selection aloud. Follow along and note that all occurrences of the /θ/ and /ð/ sounds are emphasized. You may have an opportunity to read a portion of the story in class; practice this reading by yourself as well.

From *The Night the Ghost Got In*

*Th*e ghost *th*at got into our house on *th*e night of November 17, 1915, raised such a hullabaloo of misunderstandings *th*at I am sorry I didn't just let it keep on walking, and go to bed. Its advent caused my mo*th*er to *th*row a shoe *th*rough a window of *th*e house next door and ended up wi*th* my grandfa*th*er shooting a patrolman. I am sorry, *th*erefore, as I have said, *th*at I ever paid any attention to *th*e footsteps.

*Th*ey began about a quarter past one o'clock in *th*e morning, a rhy*th*mic, quick-cadenced walking around *th*e dining-room table. My mo*th*er was asleep in one room upstairs, my bro*th*er Herman in ano*th*er; grandfa*th*er was in *th*e attic, in *th*e old walnut bed which, as you will remember, once fell on my fa*th*er.

I had just stepped out of *th*e ba*th*tub and was busily rubbing myself wi*th* a towel when I heard *th*e steps. *Th*ey were *th*e steps of a man walking rapidly around *th*e dining-room table downstairs. *Th*e light from *th*e ba*th*room shone down *th*e back steps, which dropped directly into *th*e dining-room; I could see *th*e faint shine of plates on *th*e plate-rail; I couldn't see *th*e table. *Th*e steps kept going round and round *th*e table; at regular intervals a board creaked, when it was trod upon. I supposed at first *th*at it was my fa*th*er or my bro*th*er Roy, who had gone to Indianapolis but were expected home at any time. I suspected next *th*at it was a burglar. It did not enter my mind until later *th*at it was a ghost.

—James Thurber

LESSON 7

/s/, /z/ as in sing and zero
(*Dictionary marks:* s, z)

/s/ and /z/ are both produced by placing the tip of the tongue behind, but not touching, either the lower teeth or the upper gum ridge. Use whichever tongue position gives you greater ease and accuracy, then form a slight groove along the middle of your tongue, just behind the tip. Direct a gentle stream of air along the groove. No air should escape from the sides of the tongue.

/s/ is pronounced just as /z/, except that /z/ is voiced. Place your hand securely against your larynx; begin to say /s/, prolong it, and change to /z/ without stopping, in order to feel its slight vibration as you produce the voiced sound.

I. /s/ Words

Listen to your instructor pronounce the words in the following exercises. Repeat them aloud in class and practice them afterward.

1. cent (scent)	4. seat	7. some (sum)
2. cigar	5. seed (cede)	8. soon
3. school	6. sing	9. start

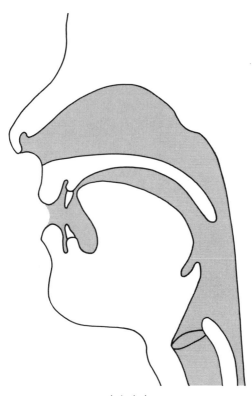

/s/ , /z/

10. still	19. last	28. horse
11. stop	20. license	29. house
12. sun (son)	21. passing	30. miss
13. also	22. perceive	31. nice
14. best	23. possible	32. once
15. deceive	24. recent	33. peace (piece)
16. eraser	25. bus	34. place
17. fasten	26. dress	35. this
18. history	27. fix	36. us

II. /z/ Words

1. zeal	11. busy	21. as
2. zebra	12. cousin	22. because
3. zenith	13. deserve	23. is
4. zero	14. dozen	24. lose
5. zest	15. easy	25. plays
6. zinc	16. fuzzy	26. please
7. zither	17. lazy	27. size
8. zodiac	18. music	28. these
9. zone	19. pleasant	29. those
10. zoo	20. usable	30. was

All of the following words end in *s*; the *s* letters in the first column are pronounced /s/, and the *s* letters in the second column are pronounced /z/.

Since the /t/ in "cats" is a voiceless sound, voiceless /s/ must follow. Since the /g/ in "dogs" is voiced, voiced /z/ must follow.

1. cats	3. boats	5. dogs	7. spoons
2. forks	4. makes	6. words	8. goes

In the following words, the *es* ending is a separate syllable, following *s* or *z*. In such words, the *es* is always pronounced /ɪz/—the /ɪ/ sound will be discussed in Lesson 12.

1. classes	3. glasses
2. courses	4. buzzes

Difficult /s/ sound combinations

1. basks	6. tasks	11. boasts	16. ghosts
2. casks	7. clasps	12. boosts	17. interests
3. flasks	8. gasps	13. casts	18. mists
4. masks	9. grasps	14. consists	19. tests
5. risks	10. lisps	15. costs	20. wrists

II. /s/ and /z/ Words and Sentences

The following words and sentences provide additional practice for you on the sounds of this lesson.

1. was, understand, say : /z/, /s/, /s/
   I was not able to understand what he had to say.
2. let's, some, ice : /s/, /s/, /s/
   Let's go to the corner for some ice cream.
3. is, fascinating, study, history : /z/, /s/, /s/, /s/
   It is fascinating to study the history of the ancient world.
4. price, gasoline, is, this, state, ours : /s/, /s/, /z/, /s/, /s/, /z/
   The price of gasoline is higher in this state than in ours.
5. house, this, best : /s/, /s/, /s/
   Which house in this part of town do you like best?
6. was, place, Sunday : /z/, /s/, /s/
   He was trying to think of a place to go on Sunday afternoon.
7. was, degrees, zero, last : /z/, /z/, /z/, /s/
   It was ten degrees below zero last January.
8. zip, this, district, is, 77266 : /z/, /s/, /s/, /z/, /s/, /s/, /s/, /s/
   The zip code of this district is 77266.
9. was, always, busy, housework : /z/, /z/, /z/, /s/
   She was always able to keep busy with her housework.
10. most, items, dozen : /s/, /z/, /z/
    Most items are cheaper by the dozen.
11. September, has, days : /s/, /z/, /z/
    September has thirty days.
12. is, this, address : /z/, /s/, /s/
    Is this your address?

III. Poetry

Listen as your instructor reads these poems aloud. Follow along and underline each occurrence of the /s/ and /z/ sounds. You may have an opportunity to read a portion of one of the poems in class. It is necessary that you practice this reading individually as well.

Peter's Little Daughter Dies

That she must change so soon her curving city;
Leave this travel scarcely started; never see
Stars again reposeful in that dear room
Where death strays not and little birds
Are never split by shot—is it like this,
Dying? Just the moment going over
The edge of body, nothing left there
That grass cannot solve?

I'd wish to settle nothing here with chisel;
No cold angel with well-fed eyes shall rest above her . . .
She once said "The Snow Queen must be very beautiful."

She was so tiny . . . She won't know what the dead are
supposed to do.

—Kenneth Patchen

The Starry Night

Faraway hands are folded and folded
or pick at the threads in the lap of blackness
or spool and spool at the tenantless tangle
of blackness, of blackness, of emptiness.

They are the stars; you can see them flash
like the bonewhite fingers of finical ladies;
and far and away the depth of their cunning
is distance—a tissue of distances.

Their heads are down; they are plummeting downwards;
we cling to our millwheel meadows; their heads

are bowed to the task; no comet commotion
of gazes effaces the emptiness.

In chairs of the rest home at paranoid random
great-aunt and great-grandmother jaw like fates
till we wish them to heaven and wake to our wishes
and cling to the earth and each other's flesh.

And ours is the flaw in the nets of blackness.
And theirs is the task by the great sea wall:
the mending, the mending, the never-mending
of blackness, of blackness, of emptiness.

—George Starbuck

LESSON 8

/l/ as in play
(*Dictionary mark:* l)

The way to produce the /l/ sound is with the tip of the tongue just above your upper front teeth, with air emerging from both sides of the raised tongue. For this sound your tongue should firmly contact the gum ridge above the upper front teeth.

I. /l/ Words

Listen to your instructor pronounce these words. Repeat them aloud in class and practice them afterward.

1. land	6. long	11. already	16. million
2. leaf	7. loss	12. believe	17. only
3. leap	8. loud	13. Billy	18. place
4. let	9. low	14. black	19. play
5. lily	10. lunar	15. hello	20. self

Be especially careful to voice /l/ at the end of words so that it will help provide good carrying power for your ideas.

1. bill	3. girl	5. owl	7. tell
2. fill	4. hill	6. pill	8. well

The /l/ sound at the end of the following words should be pronounced as a separate syllable with the pronunciation /əl/.

The /ə/ sound will be discussed in Lesson 10.

1. apple	3. little	5. table
2. bottle	4. single	6. zonal

/ l / sound at the end of one-syllable words:

1. curl	4. mule	7. school
2. fool	5. pool	8. tile
3. girl	6. rule	9. zeal

In a number of English words the letter *l* is spelled but not pronounced. Among these are almond, palm, salmon, talk, and walk.

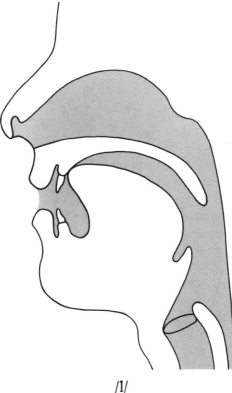

/l/

When you pronounce the following words, be certain that you say the /l/ and its adjacent consonant clearly.

1. black	7. glad	13. pledge	19. slice
2. blame	8. golf	14. plenty	20. splash
3. blur	9. mild	15. pulp	21. twelve
4. clean	10. milk	16. salt	22. wild
5. elm	11. million	17. shelve	23. wolf
6. felt	12. pleasure	18. silk	24. yelp

II. /l/ Words and Sentences

The following words and sentences provide additional practice for you on the sound of this lesson.

1. land, middle, fertile
   Most of the land in the Middle West is very fertile.
2. total, sales, volume
   The company's total sales volume was discouraging.
3. scarcely, believe, told
   He could scarcely believe what his friend told him.
4. only, class
   There were only five students in the class.
5. solid, blizzard
   The river was frozen solid during the blizzard.
6. hurriedly, telephoned
   She hurriedly telephoned her parents.
7. rule, professional, football, played
   As a rule, professional football games are played on weekends.
8. school
   The school had been in session for two weeks when he arrived.
9. shall
   I shall spend part of my vacation in New York and part in Boston.
10. bottle
    He went to get a bottle of ink.

11. novel, problem
    That's a novel approach to the problem.
12. placed, blue, table
    She placed the blue table in front of the window.

III. Poetry

When your instructor reads this poem, listen carefully and identify the /l/ sound of the lesson for class or individual practice.

Lucinda Matlock

I went to the dances at Chandlerville,
And played snap-out at Winchester.
One time we changed partners,
Driving home in the moonlight of middle June,
And then I found Davis.
We were married and lived together for seventy years,
Enjoying, working, raising the twelve children,
Eight of whom we lost
Ere I had reached the age of sixty.
I spun, I wove, I kept the house, I nursed the sick,
I made the garden, and for holiday
Rambled over the fields where sang the larks,
And by Spoon River gathering many a shell,
And many a flower and medicinal weed—
Shouting to the wooded hills, singing to the green valleys.
At ninety-six I had lived enough, that is all,
And passed to a sweet repose.
What is this I hear of sorrow and weariness,
Anger, discontent and drooping hopes?
Degenerate sons and daughters,
Life is too strong for you—
It takes life to love Life.

—Edgar Lee Masters

LESSON 9

/r/ as in already
(*Dictionary mark:* r)

The /r/ sound is made with the tip of the tongue toward the middle of the mouth but not touching the roof of the mouth. When producing the /r/ sound, take care not to pull your tongue too far back.

I. /r/ Words

Listen to your instructor pronounce these words. Repeat them aloud in class and practice them afterward. On words underlined, be certain to pronounce the vowel sound *following* the letter *r*.

1. already	10. frank	19. proud
2. around	11. hundred	20. provide
3. arrow	12. introduce	21. ready
4. borrow	13. merry	22. real
5. brown	14. prepare	23. really
6. carry	15. produce (verb)	24. red
7. children	16. promote	25. represent
8. contradict	17. pronounce	26. ride
9. dream	18. protect	27. room

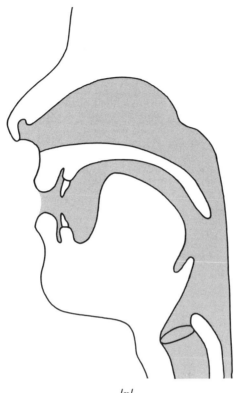

/r/

| 28. round | 30. very | 32. zero |
| 29. route | 31. wearily | |

II. Linking-/r/ Words

These phrases should contain the /r/ sound although it may seem to you that you pronounce the /r/ sound as a part of the succeeding word which begins with a vowel.

1. drive the car away
2. far away
3. far east
4. share each other's book
5. there are many
6. where are they

III. Dropped-/r/ Words

Many persons from the East and South drop the /r/ from the middle of some words and from the end of most words when the *r* is preceded by a vowel. It appears, however, that the use of the /r/ sound in the middle and at the end of words is becoming more common in all speech regions of the United States.

1. absorb	7. corn	13. harsh
2. barn	8. course	14. lord
3. board	9. force	15. pork
4. born	10. fork	16. short
5. chart	11. fourth	17. storm
6. chore	12. harm	18. sword

IV. /r/ Words and Sentences

The following words and sentences provide additional practice for you on the sound of this lesson.

1. where, are
   Where are you planning to take the examination?
2. ride, train
   It's a long ride on the train to Chicago.
3. room, from, street
   She liked to have a room away from the noise of the street.
4. grill, car, round
   The grill of the car was round.
5. relay, broke, year's, record
   The relay team broke last year's record.
6. around, rear
   Did the fence go all the way around to the rear of the house?
7. carry, trunk
   Please help me carry the trunk.

8. Republican, party
   They all belonged to the Republican Party.
9. are, trip
   Are you going to take a trip this vacation?
10. car, bright, red
    The new car was bright red.
11. cheered
    All the students cheered.
12. year, very
    This year is going by very fast.

V. Prose

When your instructor reads this story, listen carefully and identify the /r/ sound for class or individual practice.

The Rabbits Who Caused All the Trouble

Within the memory of the youngest child there was a family
of rabbits who lived near a pack of wolves. The wolves an-
nounced that they did not like the way the rabbits were living.
(The wolves were crazy about the way they themselves were
living, because it was the only way to live.) One night several
wolves were killed in an earthquake and this was blamed on the
rabbits, for it is well known that rabbits pound on the ground
with their hind legs and cause earthquakes. On another night
one of the wolves was killed by a bolt of lightning and this was
also blamed on the rabbits, for it is well known that lettuce-
eaters cause lightning. The wolves threatened to civilize the
rabbits if they didn't behave, and the rabbits decided to run
away to a desert island. But the other animals, who lived at a
great distance, shamed them, saying, "You must stay where you
are and be brave. This is no world for escapists. If the wolves
attack you, we will come to your aid, in all probability." So

the rabbits continued to live near the wolves and one day there was a terrible flood which drowned a great many wolves. This was blamed on the rabbits, for it is well known that carrot-nibblers with long ears cause floods. The wolves descended on the rabbits, for their own good, and imprisoned them in a dark cave, for their own protection.

When nothing was heard about the rabbits for some weeks, the other animals demanded to know what had happened to them. The wolves replied that the rabbits had been eaten and since they had been eaten the affair was a purely internal matter. But the other animals warned that they might possibly unite against the wolves unless some reason was given for the destruction of the rabbits. So the wolves gave them one. "They were trying to escape," said the wolves, "and, as you know, this is no world for escapists."

Moral: Run, don't walk, to the nearest desert island.

—James Thurber

LESSON 10

/ɝ /ɚ /
/ɝ/ and /ɚ/ as in w**o**rk**er**

/ə/ʌ/
/ə/ and /ʌ/ as in **a**b**o**ve
(*Dictionary marks:* ər, ə)

Following are examples of the /ɝ/ sound, as in "bird." This voiced sound is stressed, and it is always in the accented syllable of a word. In the word "curtain," the first syllable is the stressed or accented syllable. In "prefer," the last syllable is the stressed or accented syllable. The /ɝ/ sound is a vowel, not the consonant /r/ as in "run."

I. /ɝ/ Words

(Stressed and always in the accented syllable of a word)

1. *ear*ned
2. *ur*ge
3. b*ir*d
4. c*ur*tain
5. f*ir*
6. pref*er*

II. Contrasting Pairs

Consonant /r/   *Vowel* /ɝ/

1. *r*un   –   bu*r*n

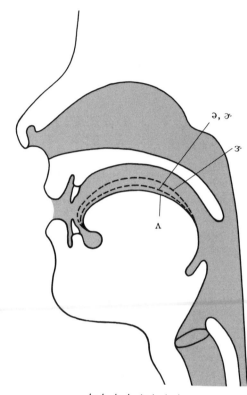

/ɝ/, /ɚ/, /ə/, /ʌ/

2. *r*oad   –   w*or*d
3. ca*r*   –   ref*er*

Following are examples of the unstressed /ɚ/ sound, as in "after." This voiced sound is always in the unaccented position of the word, but it is otherwise identical in sound to the /ɝ/ above. *Sum* in "summer" is the stressed syllable, while *er* is unstressed. The /ɚ/ sound is a vowel, not the consonant /r/ as in "run."

III. /ɚ/ Words

(Unstressed and always in the unaccented syllable of a word)

1. after
2. summer
3. better

4. yesterday
5. interfere
6. overtime

IV. Contrasting Pairs

Consonant /r/   Vowel /ɚ/

1. deplore – letter
2. fear – paper
3. around – afternoon

V. /ɝ/ and /ɚ/ Words Compared

The difference in the production of /ɝ/ and /ɚ/ is primarily that in /ɝ/ the tongue is raised and slightly tense but not strained or drawn back, while for /ɚ/ the tongue is lower and more relaxed.

Stressed /ɝ/

1. early
2. firm
3. purple
4. worry
5. worth

Unstressed /ɚ/

1. another
2. bitter
3. color
4. summertime
5. teacher

/ɝ/ words

1. burn   4. circle
2. burst   5. curl
3. certain   6. dirt

/ɚ/ words

1. afternoon   4. faster
2. butterscotch   5. hamburger
3. eagerly   6. linger

7. earth	11. learn	7. miniature	11. temperature
8. girl	12. third	8. paper	12. understand
9. heard	13. word	9. perform	13. wonderful
10. journey	14. work	10. stronger	14. younger

VI. /ɝ/ and /ɚ/ Words and Sentences

The following words and sentences provide additional practice for you on this sound.

/ɝ/ (in stressed syllables)

1. church
   The church was the tallest building in town.
2. girl
   The girl chose to attend the state college.
3. learn
   He had to learn the axiom for his math class.
4. word
   The meaning of the word has changed.

/ɚ/ (in unstressed syllables)

1. father
   His father decided against the plan.
2. letter
   She mailed the letter on Monday.
3. paper
   Each student had to type a long paper.
4. teacher
   The teacher discussed the assignment.

VII. Avoiding the "intrusive r"

Some persons from the East and South are likely to insert the r sound where it is not spelled and is not needed for linking as in Lesson 9—for example, it is improper to pronounce "law office" as if it were spelled "lore office." This is called the "intrusive r," and it should not be used to connect a word that ends in a vowel with a word that begins with a vowel.

1. china always
   Fine china always appeared on her table.
2. data in
   The data in that study are well organized.
3. drama is
   The drama is about an everyday problem.
4. drawing
   His charcoal drawing was on exhibition.

The following two sounds are /ʌ/ as in "sun," "fun," and "under," and /ə/ as in "alone," "fountain," and "surgeon." These sounds are parallel to the preceding sounds of this lesson in that /ʌ/ is always found in stressed, or accented, syllables, while /ə/ is always found in the unstressed, or unaccented, syllables.

The /ʌ/ sound is made simply by opening the mouth and voicing the sound. The /ə/ is identical in sound to /ʌ/, and is made with the same unrounded lips and a slightly more relaxed tongue.

VIII. /ʌ/ Words

(Stressed and always in the accented syllable of a word)

1. brush	9. punish
2. cover	10. rush
3. drug	11. shut
4. fun	12. some
5. judge	13. sun
6. just	14. study
7. love	15. touch
8. mushroom	16. wonder

IX. /ə/ Words

(Unstressed and always in the unaccented syllable of a word)

1. *a*lone
2. circ*u*s
3. fount*ai*n
4. preci*ou*s
5. surg*eo*n
6. tru*a*nt

X. /ʌ/ Words and Sentences

1. study, but
   He started to study, but he stopped to go and see a friend.
2. done
   The cyclone had done considerable damage.
3. us, just
   Will you tell us just where to begin?
4. much
   How much was the admission?
5. other
   I thought the other picture was better.

XI. Speech

Listen as your instructor reads this selection aloud. Follow along and underline each occurrence of the /ɝ/, /ɚ/, /ə/, and /ʌ/ sounds. You may have an opportunity to read a portion of the selection in class; practice this reading by yourself as well.

From *Othello* (Act V, Scene 2)

Othello: Soft you! a word or two before you go.
   I have done the state some service, and they know't.
   No more of that. I pray you, in your letters,
   When you shall these unlucky deeds relate,
   Speak of me as I am. Nothing extenuate,
   Nor set down aught in malice. Then must you speak

Of one that loved not wisely, but too well;
Of one not easily jealous, but, being wrought,
Perplexed in the extreme; of one whose hand,
Like the base Judean, threw a pearl away
Richer than all his tribe; of one whose subdued eyes,
Albeit unusèd to the melting mood,
Drop tears as fast as the Arabian trees
Their medicinal gum. Set you down this.
And say besides that in Aleppo once,
Where a malignant and a turbaned Turk
Beat a Venetian and traduced the state,
I took by th' throat the circumcisèd dog
And smote him—thus.
    [*He stabs himself.*]

        .   .   .

I kissed thee ere I killed thee. No way but this,
Killing myself, to die upon a kiss.

—William Shakespeare

LESSON 11

/m/ as in *m*ade
/n/ as in *n*ow
/ŋ/ as in si*ng*
(*Dictionary marks:* m, n, ng,
and sometimes ŋ for ng)

To make the /m/ sound, put your lips together and produce the voiced sound.

The /n/ sound is made with the tip of the tongue touching the gum ridge just above the upper front teeth; it is also a voiced sound.

The third sound of this lesson, the voiced /ŋ/ sound, which never occurs at the beginning of a word in English, is made with the back of the tongue raised.

These three nasal sounds are the only ones that are produced with air coming through the nose. Pronouncing these sounds clearly will help your listener understand you. Remember *not* to make these sounds short.

I. /m/, /n/, and /ŋ/ Words

Listen to your instructor pronounce these words. Repeat them aloud in class and practice them afterward.

1. mark   2. medical   3. almost

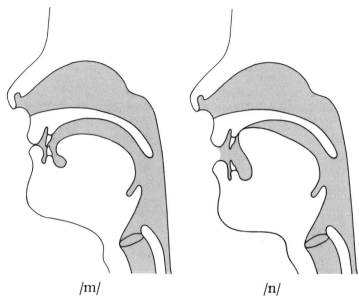

/m/

/n/

4. famous
5. lamb
6. name
7. blossom
8. new (knew)
9. knife
10. only
11. panel
12. fine
13. garden
14. town
15. anger
16. bank
17. singer
18. think
19. morning
20. spring
21. thing

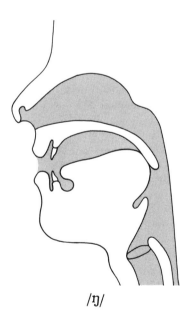

/ŋ/

II. Problem /ŋ/ Words and Sentences

Words ending in "-ing" (use /ɪŋ/, not /ɪn/)

1. falling
2. pulling
3. running
4. talking
5. walking
6. Are they coming with you?
7. Are you going with me?

Except in specific cases, the /ŋ/ sound should not be followed by a /k/ sound or by any kind of click. Like /m/ and /n/, the /ŋ/ sound can be prolonged by the voice.

Words spelled with "-ngth" (use /ŋk/ not /n/)

1. length
2. strength
3. lengthen
4. strengthen

III. Words Pronounced with /ŋ/ Only

Any word ending in the spelling "-ng" or "-ngue"

1. bring
2. fling
3. gong
4. hang
5. king
6. sing
7. song
8. spring
9. tongue
10. wrong
11. harangue
12. meringue

Any word ending in "-ng" or "-ngue" *plus a suffix*

1. hanger
2. hanging
3. kingly
4. ringing
5. singing
6. springing
7. winging
8. haranguing

IV. /ŋ/ plus /g/ Words

Adjectives of the comparative and superlative degrees

/ŋ/	long	strong	young
/ŋg/	longer	stronger	younger
/ŋg/	longest	strongest	youngest

Common /ŋ/ plus /g/ words; pronounce both sounds.

1. anger	7. finger	13. language	19. singly
2. angry	8. hunger	14. linger	20. spangle
3. bongo	9. hungry	15. mangled	21. tangle
4. Congo	10. jangle	16. mingle	22. tango
5. dangle	11. jingle	17. mongrel	23. tingle
6. English	12. jungle	18. single	24. wrangle

V. /m/, /n/, /ŋ/, and /ŋg/ Words and Sentences

In the first four sentences you will note words that include the /ŋ/ plus /g/ sounds which you have just practiced. Beginning with the fifth sentence, you have additional drill on the nasal sounds of this lesson.

1. scientists, English, language
   Scientists add words to the English language every day.
2. young, children, mingled
   The young children mingled happily with the crowd.
3. finger, preparing, dinner
   She cut her finger preparing dinner.
4. youngest, in, strongest
   The youngest boy in the class was the strongest.
5. governor, assigned, men
   The governor assigned three men to the project.

6. Boston, in, almost
   He was able to drive to Boston in almost four hours.
7. know, length, Long Island
   Do you know the length of Long Island?
8. entire, skyline, from, window
   You are able to see the entire skyline from this window.
9. notebook, in
   He put his notebook in his pocket.
10. running, alongside
    The dog was running alongside the car.
11. bring, newspaper, home
    I wish you would bring the newspaper home with you.
12. need, another, hanger, in
    Do we need another hanger in that closet?

VI. Poetry

Listen as your instructor reads these two poems aloud. Follow along and underline each occurrence of the /m/, /n/, and /ŋ/ sounds. You may have an opportunity to read a portion of the poems in class; practice them by yourself as well.

Do Not Go Gentle into That Good Night

Do not go gentle into that good night,
Old age should burn and rave at close of day;
Rage, rage against the dying of the light.

Though wise men at their end know dark is right,
Because their words had forked no lightning they
Do not go gentle into that good night.

Good men, the last wave by, crying how bright
Their frail deeds might have danced in a green bay,
Rage, rage against the dying of the light.

THE SOUNDS OF AMERICAN ENGLISH

Wild men who caught and sang the sun in flight,
And learn, too late, they grieved it on its way,
Do not go gentle into that good night.

Grave men, near death, who see with blinding sight
Blind eyes could blaze like meteors and be gay,
Rage, rage against the dying of the light.

And you, my father, there on the sad height,
Curse, bless, me now with your fierce tears, I pray.
Do not go gentle into that good night.
Rage, rage against the dying of the light.

—Dylan Thomas

Prelude I

The winter evening settles down
With smell of steaks in passageways.
Six o'clock.
The burnt-out ends of smoky days.
And now a gusty shower wraps
The grimy scraps
Of withered leaves about your feet
And newspapers from vacant lots;
The showers beat
On broken blinds and chimney-pots,
And at the corner of the street
A lonely cab-horse steams and stamps.
And then the lighting of the lamps.

—T. S. Eliot

LESSON 12

/ɪ/ as in *in*
/i/ as in *each*
(*Dictionary marks:* i, ē)

Both vowels /ɪ/ and /i/ are voiced with the tongue well forward and high in the mouth. /i/ usually seems to be the longer sound, and it is made with the tongue and lips somewhat tense.

/ɪ/ is a short sound made with relaxed tongue and lips.

/ɪ/ and /i/, although different sounds, are similar in sound and production.

I. /ɪ/ and /i/ Words

Listen to your instructor pronounce these words. Repeat them aloud in class and practice them afterward.

1. it	4. eat	7. Cincinnati	10. Mississippi
2. fit	5. feet (feat)	8. macaroni	11. Missouri
3. lid	6. lead	9. Miami	12. spaghetti

II. Contrasting Pairs

Your instructor will pronounce the following pairs of words and sentences for you to repeat aloud in class and practice when you are alone. Note that the sounds of this lesson are italicized.

1. *mitt – meat* : /ɪ/ – /i/
   The mitt was burned in the fire.
   The meat was burned in the fire.
2. *since* – sense : /ɪ/ – /ɛ/
   I haven't seen you since last summer.
   It doesn't make much sense.
3. *been* – Ben : /ɪ/ – /ɛ/
   I've been to the movies.
   My friend, Ben, went with me.
4. *itch – each* : /ɪ/ – /i/
   The poison ivy itch is painful.
   We will each bring fifty cents.
5. *tinder* – tender : /ɪ/ – /ɛ/
   The tinderbox is by the fireplace.
   The roast was tender.

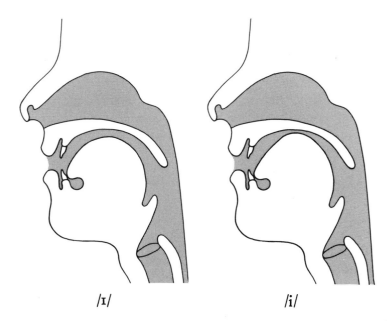

/ɪ/　　　　　　　　/i/

6. *rid* – red : /ɪ/ – /ɛ/
Get rid of your old clothes.
Get red paint, please.
7. *bee* – bay : /i/ – /eɪ/
The biology class finished a unit on the bee.
There were many boats in the bay.
8. *pill* – *peel* : /ɪ/ – /i/
It was a bitter pill.
He slipped on the apple peel.

III. /ɪ/ Words

1. inch	9. condition	17. sheriff
2. irrigate	10. fishing	18. similar
3. itch	11. him (hymn)	19. since
4. addition	12. milk	20. spirit
5. ambition	13. minister	21. superstition
6. been (bin)	14. miracle	22. syrup
7. children	15. mirror	23. wish
8. cling	16. religious	24. women

In the next exercise, note what happens to some /ɪ/ sounds. If you pronounce "city" or "pretty" alone, you may hear the last sound as /i/. If you use these words in a sentence such as "The city is pretty tonight," the last sound is /ɪ/. In most cases this change of sound is due to less stress or accentuation for the final sound in context.

IV. /ɪ/ Words and Sentences

1. city, is, pretty
The city is pretty tonight.
2. instead, going, Missouri, Mississippi
Instead of going to Missouri, he went to Mississippi.
3. imagine, it, study
She tried to imagine what it would be like to study abroad.

4. will, it, if, him
   Will he do it if I ask him?
5. spilled, ink
   I spilled some ink on the book.
6. is, it, going, this
   Is it going to rain this afternoon?
7. in, addition, in, bill
   There was an error in addition in the bill.
8. his, trip
   His car broke down on the trip to New York.

V. /i/ Words and Sentences

1. keep, creek, legal
   If they don't keep the creek from becoming polluted, we'll turn to legal enforcement.
2. easy
   Did you think that examination was easy?
3. debris
   The park was filled with debris.
4. feet
   His feet were injured in the accident.
5. agree
   Do you agree with him?
6. asleep, sea
   He fell asleep to the sound of the sea.
7. need, key
   We need a special key to open the door.
8. three, speech
   There were three points in the President's speech.

VI. Poetry

Listen as your instructor reads these poems aloud. Follow along, and note that in the first poem all occurrences of the

/ɪ/ and /i/ sounds are emphasized. You may have an opportunity to read a portion of one of the poems in class; practice this reading by yourself as well.

The Missing Person

He has come to report himself
A missing person.

The authorities
Hand him the forms.

He knows how they have waited
With the learned patience of barbers

In small shops, idle,
Stropping their razors.

But now that these spaces in his life
Stare up at him blankly,

Waiting to be filled in,
He does not know where to begin.

Afraid
That he cannot answer even

To a description of himself,
He asks for a mirror.

They reassure him
That he can be nowhere

But wherever he finds himself
From moment to moment,

Which, for the moment, is here.
And he might like to believe them,

But in the mirror
He sees what is missing.

It *is* h*i*mself
H*e* s*ee*s there *e*merg*i*ng

Slowly, as from the dark
Of a furn*i*shed room,

Onl*y* when *it is* dark,
One who r*ecei*ves no mail

And *is* known to the landlady onl*y*
For k*ee*p*i*ng h*i*mself to h*i*mself,

And for whom *it* w*i*ll b*e* y*ea*rs yet
B*e*fore h*e* can trust to the light

Th*is* last d*i*sguise, h*i*mself.

— Donald Justice

So Run Along and Play

You might think I was in the way.
So run along—along with what?
There isn't much that I have got
To run along with or beside.
The door, of course, is open wide;
The day, of course, is clear and fine;
The time right now, I guess, is mine.

But what is there to run to?
It wouldn't be much fun to
Run along—well, just to run.
O.K. for two or three; I'm *one*,
I'm all alone. I guess I'll walk
Along. I'll stop somewhere and talk;
Perhaps I'll think where I can walk to,
Because that's where there's what I'll talk to.

I'll walk along, but I won't play;
I won't play I am playing. Way
Beyond the third house one block back's
Another house with funny cracks
Across the paint. It seems to me
That's where some painter ought to be.

He should have been there years ago;
Maybe they don't like painters, though.
Or maybe he has my complaint:
They said "So run along and paint."
Well, if he ran along like me,
I'll bet I may know where he'll be.

—David McCord

LESSON 13

/eɪ/ as in m*a*y
/oʊ/ as in *o*ld
/ɔɪ/ as in b*o*y
(*Dictionary marks:* ā, ō, ȯi)

All three of these sounds, /eɪ/, /oʊ/, and /ɔɪ/, are diphthongs, meaning two vowel sounds in one syllable, and are made with the tongue gliding from one sound and position to another sound and position.

/eɪ/ is produced tensely with the tip of the tongue moving smoothly but rapidly from a medium low to a higher position.

/oʊ/ is produced tensely with the lips rounding and with the back of the tongue moving slightly upward.

/ɔɪ/ is produced at the beginning with the tongue low and lips rounded; in the second element of the diphthong the tongue is raised and the lips slightly spread.

All three sounds of this lesson are voiced. Your full vocalization of these diphthongs will help to provide good carrying power for your voice.

Remember that the air should not come through your nose when you produce these diphthongs.

I. /eɪ/ Words

Listen to your instructor pronounce these words. Repeat
them aloud in class and practice
them afterward.

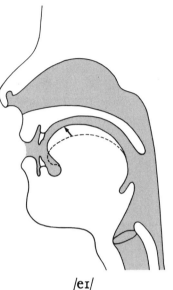

1. able
2. afraid
3. aid
4. ailment
5. ate (eight)
6. eighty
7. break (brake)
8. fate
9. gain
10. gauge
11. lame
12. paper
13. hey (hay)
14. pay
15. pray (prey)
16. stay
17. take
18. way (weigh)

/eɪ/

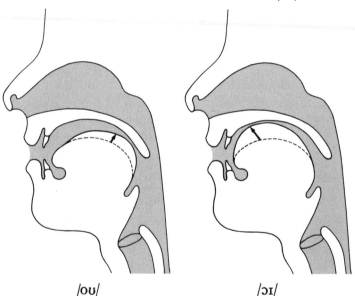

/oʊ/   /ɔɪ/

THE SOUNDS OF AMERICAN ENGLISH

II. /eɪ/ Words and Sentences

Your instructor will pronounce the following words and sentences for you to repeat aloud in class and practice when you are alone.

1. able
   When will the student be able to come to class?
2. neighbor, agent
   Our neighbor is an insurance agent.
3. they, aid
   They asked us to aid the needy family.
4. ate, train
   We ate our dinner hurriedly to catch the train.
5. name
   I signed my name to the petition.
6. paper
   Her letter filled three sheets of paper.

III. /oʊ/ Words

1. oak	7. boat	13. bow
2. ocean	8. don't	14. hoe
3. oh	9. door	15. low
4. only	10. known	16. tableau
5. open	11. moldy	17. though
6. own	12. store	18. toe

Be sure to sound the /oʊ/ in the final syllable of these words.

1. borrow	6. piano
2. fellow	7. pillow
3. follow	8. potato
4. hollow	9. tomorrow
5. narrow	10. window

IV. /oʊ/ Words and Sentences

The following words and sentences provide additional practice for you on this sound.

1. cold
   Do you like cold weather?
2. own
   Do you own a college dictionary?
3. over, ocean
   There is a hurricane over the ocean today.
4. wrote
   He wrote his first book when he was twenty-five.
5. window
   The window was dirty after the rain.
6. yellow, rose
   The yellow rose is a beautiful flower.

V. /o/ and /e/ Words

In some words such as "obey," "omit," and "notation," the /oʊ/ is very short. Only the most highly trained ear, however, will respond to this contrast between the /o/ in "obey" and the longer /oʊ/ sound in "old," which is one of the key words of this lesson.

The /e/ in "bacon" and "chaotic" and the first /e/ in "vacation" are also short sounds when contrasted carefully with the longer /eɪ/ sound in "may," which is one of the key words of this lesson.

/ o /	/ e /
1. obey	1. bacon
2. omit	2. chaotic
3. notation	3. vacation

VI. /ɔɪ/ Words

1. oil	6. coil	11. moisture	16. void
2. ointment	7. coin	12. point	17. annoy
3. oyster	8. join	13. poison	18. deploy
4. boil	9. joint	14. soil	19. enjoy
5. choice	10. loyal	15. voice	20. joy

VII. /ɔɪ/ Words and Sentences

The following words and sentences provide additional practice for you on this sound.

1. coin
   He subscribed to *The Coin Collector.*
2. point
   I was glad he raised that point in the discussion.
3. voice
   A network announcer should have a pleasant voice.
4. boiled
   Do you like boiled lobster?
5. annoy
   Doesn't the TV annoy you when it's too loud?
6. destroy
   Be sure you don't destroy your class notes.

VIII. Poetry

Listen as your instructor reads this poem aloud. Follow along and note all occurrences of the diphthongs of this lesson. You may have an opportunity to read a portion of the poem in class; practice this reading by yourself as well.

Eighteen Sixty-One

Arm'd year—year of the struggle,
No dainty rhymes or sentimental love verses for you
   terrible year,
Not you as some pale poetling seated at a desk lisping
   cadenzas piano,
But as a strong man erect, clothed in blue clothes,
   advancing, carrying a rifle on your shoulder,
With well-gristled body and sunburnt face and hands,
   with a knife in the belt at your side,
As I heard you shouting loud, your sonorous voice ringing
   across the continent,
Your masculine voice O year, as rising amid the great cities,
Amid the men of Manhattan I saw you as one of the
   workmen, the dwellers in Manhattan,
Or with large steps crossing the prairies out of Illinois and
   Indiana,
Rapidly crossing the West with springy gait and descending
   the Alleghanies,
Or down from the great lakes or in Pennsylvania, or on
   deck along the Ohio river,
Or southward along the Tennessee or Cumberland rivers,
   or at Chattanooga on the mountain top,
Saw I your gait and saw I your sinewy limbs clothed in
   blue, bearing weapons, robust year,
Heard your determin'd voice launch'd forth again and
   again,
Year that suddenly sang by the mouths of the round-lipp'd
   cannon,
I repeat you, hurrying, crashing, sad, distracted year.

                                        —Walt Whitman

LESSON 14

/k/, /g/ as in *k*itten and *g*arden
/f/, /v/ as in *f*ace and *v*ery
/p/, /b/ as in *p*aper and *b*ack
(*Dictionary marks:* k, g, f, v, p, b)

/k/ and /g/ are made the same way. The back of the tongue is raised and then lowered very quickly. The pronunciation of this pair of consonants involves an "explosion" of air. Because they cannot be prolonged, you must pronounce these sounds precisely. Pronunciation of /k/ and /g/ is sometimes followed by a small "puff" of air.

The difference between /k/ and /g/ is that /k/ is voiceless while /g/ is voiced in the larynx. It is difficult to feel the slight vibration of the larynx as you produce /g/ because of its short duration.

I. /k/ and /g/ Words

Listen to your instructor pronounce these words. Repeat them aloud in class and practice them afterward.

/k/ words

1. calm	3. cat	5. column	7. count
2. can	4. chasm	6. corps (core)	8. coupon

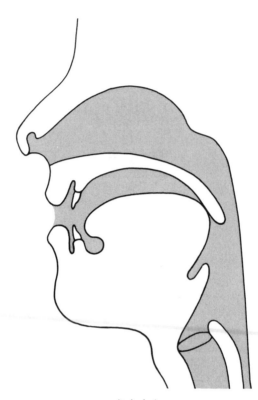

/k/, /g/

9. cow	12. adjective	15. facsimile	18. picture
10. key (quay)	13. architect	16. fact	19. risked
11. accompanist	14. discover	17. luxury	20. ask

/g/ words

1. garden	6. gown	11. asparagus	16. cog
2. gas	7. grevious	12. congratulate	17. dig
3. gather	8. guarantee	13. figure	18. flag
4. gauze	9. guard	14. hungry	19. rogue
5. gone	10. guess	15. recognize	20. vague

II. Contrasting Pairs

Your instructor will pronounce the following pairs of words and sentences for you to repeat aloud in class and practice when you are alone. Note that the word has one meaning when the final sound is the voiceless /k/, and it has a different meaning when the final sound is the voiced /g/.

1. luck – lug
   They had good luck with their project.
   They had to lug their suitcases.
2. rack – rag
   Put the books on the rack.
   Use that rag to clean the floor.
3. knack – nag
   He had a knack for carpentry.
   The old nag had once been a fine mare.
4. sack – sag
   The boy was told to sack the potatoes.
   After the blast, the floor began to sag.
5. snack – snag
   He went to the kitchen for a snack.
   He hit a snag in his homework.

The next two consonants are the voiceless /f/ and the voiced /v/. Unlike /k/ and /g/, the /f/ and /v/ sounds may be prolonged. To form these sounds, the lower lip contacts the upper teeth while air comes between them. Do you feel the vibration from the friction of the air against your teeth and lower lip?

To make certain you are voicing the /v/ sound, put your hand securely against your larynx in order to feel its slight vibration as you produce the voiced sound.

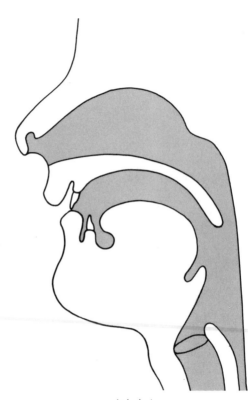

/f/, /v/

III. /f/ and /v/ Words

/f/ words

1. family	7. coughs	13. cough
2. February	8. diphtheria	14. enough
3. feed	9. fifth	15. knife
4. first	10. infamous	16. laugh
5. phenomena	11. prophet	17. mastiff
6. phenomenon	12. significant	18. relief

THE SOUNDS OF AMERICAN ENGLISH

/v/ words

1. variety	5. gloves	9. relevant	13. believe
2. victual	6. hover	10. removes	14. leave
3. view	7. leaves	11. shoves	15. love
4. vowel	8. moves	12. woven	16. strive

IV. Contrasting Pairs

Your instructor will pronounce the following pairs of words and sentences for you to repeat aloud in class and practice when you are alone. Note that the voiceless /f/ sound and the voiced /v/ sound change meaning in certain words.

1. half – halve
   I'll give you half of my apple.
   Use the knife to halve the apple.
2. safe – save
   Is it safe to walk there alone at night?
   Save that coin until we check its value.
3. grief – grieve
   There was much grief for the old man.
   Did Margaret grieve long for her father?
4. proof – prove
   I'll have to see your proof first.
   If you can prove that theorem, you pass the test.
5. belief – believe
   That belief is out of date.
   Do you believe that they will succeed?

The third pair of consonants is the voiceless /p/ and the voiced /b/. To produce these sounds, the lips are brought together and then are separated very quickly.

It is easy to hear and feel the explosion of air for these sounds. A small "puff" of air follows the pronunciation of /p/ and /b/.

It is difficult to feel the slight vibration of the larynx as you produce /b/ because of its short duration.

Remember that you must pronounce the sounds /p/ and /b/ precisely.

V. /p/ and /b/ Words

/p/ words

1. percolate	7. apron	13. develop
2. perform	8. hospital	14. group
3. perspiration	9. omnipotent	15. limp
4. poem	10. separate	16. rope
5. prediction	11. surprise	17. ship
6. pretty	12. jumper	18. wipe

/b/ words

1. bear (bare)	6. absurd	11. drab
2. because	7. fable	12. herb
3. bronchial	8. liberty	13. prescribe
4. burst	9. robber	14. rib
5. bout	10. symbol	15. sob

VI. Contrasting Pairs

Your instructor will pronounce the following pairs of words and sentences for you to repeat aloud in class and practice when you are alone. Note that the word has one meaning when the final sound is the voiceless /p/ and another meaning when the final sound is the voiced /b/.

1. cap – cab
   He bought a cap at the store.
   He caught a cab at the corner.

2. lap – lab
   He won on the last lap.
   I'll meet you after chemistry lab.
3. nap – nab
   Will the baby nap long?
   Will they nab the leader?
4. tap – tab
   Tap him on the shoulder.
   Tab those folders correctly.

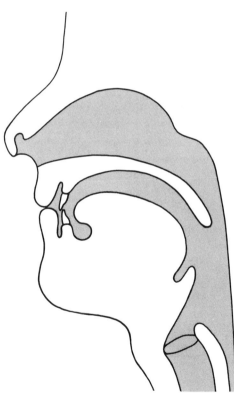

/p/, /b/

VII. Scene

Your instructor may request two students to act this scene. In addition, you should read the scene aloud and carefully evaluate your pronunciation of the consonants studied in the lesson.

The Importance of Being Earnest (from Act I)

Lady Bracknell: You can take a seat, Mr. Worthing.

Jack: Thank you, Lady Bracknell, I prefer standing.

Lady Bracknell: I feel bound to tell you that you are not down on my list of eligible young men, although I have the same list as the dear Duchess of Bolton has. We work together, in fact. However, I am quite ready to enter your name, should your answers be what a really affectionate mother requires. Do you smoke?

Jack: Well, yes, I must admit I smoke.

Lady Bracknell: I am glad to hear it. A man should always have an occupation of some kind. There are far too many idle men in London as it is. How old are you?

Jack: Twenty-nine.

Lady Bracknell: A very good age to be married at. I have always been of the opinion that a man who desires to get married should know either everything or nothing. Which do you know?

Jack: I know nothing, Lady Bracknell.

Lady Bracknell: I am pleased to hear it. I do not approve of anything that tampers with natural ignorance. Ignorance is like a delicate exotic fruit; touch it and the bloom is gone. The whole theory of modern education is radically unsound. Fortunately in England, at any rate, education produces no effect whatsoever. If it did, it would prove a serious danger to the upper classes, and probably lead to acts of violence in Grosvenor Square. What is your income?

Jack: Between seven and eight thousand a year.

Lady Bracknell: In land, or in investments?

Jack: In investments, chiefly.

Lady Bracknell: That is satisfactory. What between the duties expected of one during one's lifetime, and the duties exacted from one after one's death, land has ceased to be either a profit or a pleasure. It gives one position, and prevents one from keeping it up. That's all that can be said about land.

Jack: I have a country house with some land, of course, attached to it, about fifteen hundred acres, I believe; but I don't depend on that for my real income. In fact, as far as I can make out, the poachers are the only people who make anything out of it.

Lady Bracknell: A country house! How many bedrooms? Well, that point can be cleared up afterwards. You have a town house, I hope? A girl with a simple, unspoiled nature, like Gwendolen, could hardly be expected to reside in the country.

Jack: Well, I own a house in Belgrave Square, but it is let by the year to Lady Bloxham. Of course, I can get it back whenever I like, at six months' notice.

Lady Bracknell: Lady Bloxham? I don't know her.

Jack: Oh, she goes about very little. She is a lady considerably advanced in years.

Lady Bracknell: Ah, nowadays that is no guarantee of respectability of character. What number in Belgrave Square?

Jack: 149.

Lady Bracknell: The unfashionable side. I thought there was something. However, that could easily be altered.

Jack: Do you mean the fashion, or the side?

Lady Bracknell: Both, if necessary, I presume. What are your politics?

Jack: Well, I am afraid I really have none. I am a Liberal Unionist.

Lady Bracknell: Oh, they count as Tories. They dine with us.

Or come in the evening, at any rate. Now to minor matters. Are your parents living?

Jack: I have lost both my parents.

Lady Bracknell: To lose one parent, Mr. Worthing, may be regarded as a misfortune; to lose both looks like carelessness. Who was your father? He was evidently a man of some wealth. Was he born in what the Radical papers call the purple of commerce, or did he rise from the ranks of the aristocracy?

Jack: I am afraid I really don't know. The fact is, Lady Bracknell, I said I had lost my parents. It would be nearer the truth to say that my parents seem to have lost me.... I don't actually know who I am by birth. I was ... well, I was found.

Lady Bracknell: Found!

Jack: The late Mr. Thomas Cardew, an old gentleman of a very charitable and kindly disposition, found me, and gave me the name of Worthing, because he happened to have a first-class ticket for Worthing in his pocket at the time. Worthing is a place in Sussex. It is a seaside resort.

Lady Bracknell: Where did the charitable gentleman who had a first-class ticket for this seaside resort find you?

Jack: In a hand-bag.

Lady Bracknell: A hand-bag?

Jack: Yes, Lady Bracknell. I was in a hand-bag—a somewhat large, black leather hand-bag, with handles to it—an ordinary hand-bag in fact.

Lady Bracknell: In what locality did this Mr. James, or Thomas, Cardew come across this ordinary hand-bag?

Jack: In the cloak-room at Victoria Station. It was given to him in mistake for his own.

Lady Bracknell: The cloak-room at Victoria Station?

Jack: Yes. The Brighton line.

Lady Bracknell: The line is immaterial. Mr. Worthing, I confess I feel somewhat bewildered by what you have just told me. To be born, or at any rate bred, in a hand-bag, whether it had handles or not, seems to me to display a contempt for the ordinary decencies of family life that remind one of the worst excesses of the French Revolution. And I presume you know what that unfortunate movement led to? As for the particular locality in which the hand-bag was found, a cloak-room at a railway station might serve to conceal a social indiscretion—has probably, indeed, been used for that purpose before now—but it could hardly be regarded as an assured basis for a recognized position in good society.

Jack: May I ask you then what you would advise me to do? I need hardly say I would do anything in the world to ensure Gwendolen's happiness.

Lady Bracknell: I would strongly advise you, Mr. Worthing, to try and acquire some relations as soon as possible, and to make a definite effort to produce at any rate one parent, of either sex, before the season is quite over.

Jack: Well, I don't see how I could possibly manage to do that. I can produce the hand-bag at any moment. It is in my dressing-room at home. I really think that should satisfy you, Lady Bracknell.

Lady Bracknell: Me, sir! What has it to do with me? You can hardly imagine that I and Lord Bracknell would dream of allowing our only daughter—a girl brought up with the utmost care—to marry into a cloak-room, and form an alliance with a parcel? Good morning, Mr. Worthing!

—Oscar Wilde

LESSON 15

/w/ as in *w*ait
/hw/ as in *wh*isper
(*Dictionary marks:* w, hw)

Read the following sentences aloud: "Whether the weather is good or not, we'll go to the game." "That's where I'm going to wear my new coat."

Did you make a distinction between "whether" and "weather" and between "where" and "wear"?

The two sounds in this lesson are /w/ as in "wait" and /hw/ as in "whisper."

/w/ is produced by rounding the lips, and then separating them with a little exhalation of air.

The sound closest to /w/ is /hw/. In the /hw/ sound, a small puff of air precedes the /w/. Put your hand about an inch from your mouth and say /hw/. Do you feel the puff at the beginning of the sound? Exhale the puff of air easily.

I. /w/ Words

Listen to your instructor pronounce these words. Repeat them aloud in class and practice them afterward.

1. weak (week)	4. west	7. awake
2. wedge	5. wonderful	8. away (aweigh)
3. weigh (way)	6. anyway	9. backward

| 10. forward | 12. sandwich | 14. twice |
| 11. quick | 13. square | 15. upward |

II. /w/ Words and Sentences

Your instructor will pronounce the following pairs of words and the sentences for you to repeat aloud in class and practice when you are alone.

1. walk
   I decided to walk to school this afternoon.

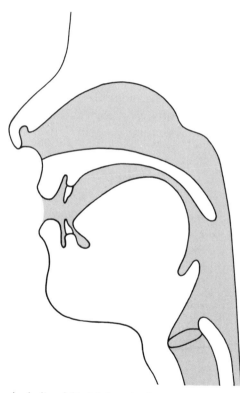

/w/, /hw/ (Initial articulatory position)

2. always, homework

   He always put off doing his homework.

3. forward

   The general gave the command, "Forward!"

4. reward

   The FBI offered a reward for information about the bank robber.

5. unwise

   That might be an unwise plan.

6. watch

   As the car sped around the corner, the man yelled "Watch out!"

III. /hw/ Words

Listen to your instructor pronounce these words. Repeat them aloud in class and practice them afterward. Keep your hand about an inch in front of your mouth as you practice the words in order to check the /h/ sound element.

1. what	6. whip	11. anywhere
2. wheat	7. whisper	12. awhile
3. wheel	8. whistle	13. meanwhile
4. where	9. white	14. overwhelm
5. while	10. whittle	15. somewhere

Many speakers say /w/ instead of /hw/; for example, /wat/ instead of "what," /wɪspɚ/ instead of "whisper"; the /hw/ seems to be disappearing from the speech of even careful speakers. However, if you want clear pronunciation that will be accepted by educated people everywhere, always pronounce every word spelled *wh* as /hw/. The exceptions are "who" and "whole," plus their derivatives, such as "whoever," "whom," and "wholesome." The first sound of these words is the /h/ sound, or simply an exhalation of air.

IV. /h/ Words Spelled "wh-"

1. who   2. whoever   3. whole   4. wholesome   5. whom

V. Contrasting Pairs

The following words provide additional practice for you on the sounds of this lesson. Note that the meaning of a word may depend on distinguishing the /w/ and /hw/ sounds.

1.	wail	– whale
2.	watt	– what
3.	way (weigh)	– whey
4.	we (wee)	– whee
5.	wear	– where
6.	weather	– whether
7.	wet	– whet
8.	wile	– while
9.	wine	– whine
10.	witch	– which

In the next contrast drill, note that the word containing the /hw/ sound is italicized.

1. wail – *whale*
   The seabird's wail warned us of the whale.
2. wet – *whetstone*
   A wet whetstone sharpens best.
3. *where* – wear
   That's where I'm going to wear my new coat.
4. *whether* – weather
   Whether or not the weather is good, we'll go to the game.
5. *what* – watt
   What else do we need besides two 100-watt bulbs?
6. *which* – witch
   Which witch won the Halloween prize?

7. *whine* – wine

The whine of the grape press meant wine-making time.

VI. Poetry

Listen as your instructor reads these two poems aloud. Follow along and note that all occurrences of the /w/ and /hw/ sounds are emphasized. You may have an opportunity to read a portion of one of the poems in class; practice this reading by yourself as well.

She Walks in Beauty

She *w*alks in beauty, like the night
  Of cloudless climes and starry skies;
And all that's best of dark and bright
  Meet in her aspect and her eyes:
Thus mellowed to that tender light
  *Wh*ich heaven to gaudy day denies.

One shade the more, one ray the less,
  Had half impaired the nameless grace
*Wh*ich *w*aves in every raven tress,
  Or softly lightens o'er her face;
*Wh*ere thoughts serenely s*w*eet express
  How pure, how dear their d*w*elling place.

And on that cheek, and o'er that brow,
  So soft, so calm, yet elo*qu*ent,
The smiles that *w*in, the tints that glow,
  But tell of days in goodness spent,
A mind at peace *w*ith all below,
  A heart whose love is innocent!

—Byron

The Watcher

The dog who knew the winter felt no spleen
And sat indoors; the birds made tracks all day
Across the blue-*wh*ite crust; he *w*atched the branches s*w*ay
Like grasping fingers mirrored on the snow.
The house *w*as *w*arm, and long ago the grass *w*as green;
And all day long bones rattled in his head,
*Wh*ile seven *w*ithered apples s*w*ung like time,
So q*u*ick, so short the pendulum. The tree,
Cursing *w*ith *w*ind, prayed mercy on its knee.
He saw the snow toward evening flush to red,
Stepped on his bowl of milk, licked up his crime,
Rolled on his cozy self and smelled his skin,
And snuffed the nighttime out around the bed.

—Ruth Stone

LESSON 16

/u/ as in do
/ʊ/ as in look
(*Dictionary marks:* ü, u̇)

Your ears perceive /ʊ/ and /u/ as almost the same sound, and your speech mechanism makes /ʊ/ and /u/ in almost the same way. Both vowels are voiced with the back of the tongue raised and the lips rounded. /u/ is usually the longer sound, with the lips well rounded. /ʊ/ is a short sound with the lips somewhat less rounded.

I. /u/ and /ʊ/ Words

/u/

1. ooze	4. tomb	7. grew	10. loom
2. cool	5. whose	8. shoe	11. true
3. rule	6. blue (blew)	9. through	12. woo

/ʊ/

1. book	5. full	9. shook	13. tourist
2. bush	6. good	10. should	14. wood (would)
3. could	7. push	11. stood	15. woof
4. cushion	8. put	12. took	16. wool

96

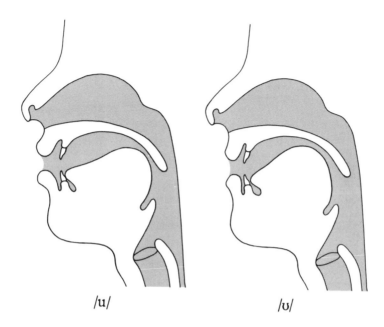

/u/   /ʊ/

II. Contrasting Pairs

Your instructor will pronounce the following pairs of words and sentences for you to repeat aloud in class and practice when you are alone. Note that the word has one meaning when the middle sound is /u/ and another meaning if it is changed to /ʊ/.

1. Luke – look
   My uncle's name was Luke.
   Let's take another look.
2. pool – pull
   The diving board was at the other end of the pool.
   He gave the rope a hard pull.
3. fool – full
   He doesn't fool me a bit.
   The cup was full to the top.

4. wooed – wood

He wooed her in the garden.

The wood soaked in the rain for hours.

III. /ʊ/ and /u/ Words and Sentences

The following words and sentences provide additional practice
for you on the sounds of this lesson.

1. book /ʊ/

   He asked us to return the reference book.
2. move /u/

   Move this desk to the other side.
3. push /ʊ/

   He tried to push the piano.
4. drew /u/

   The engineer drew a map of the city.
5. would /ʊ/

   I would like to make a dental appointment.
6. shouldn't /ʊ/

   They shouldn't have gone out in the storm.
7. through /u/

   Don't go through that tunnel.
8. wool /ʊ/

   I liked the wool suit best.
9. rule /u/

   Is this rule fair to everyone?
10. cook /ʊ/

    The cook prepared my favorite dessert.

IV. Poetry

Listen as your instructor reads this poem aloud. Follow along
and note that all occurrences of the /ʊ/ sound are emphasized.

You may have an opportunity to read a portion of the poem in class; practice this reading by yourself as well.

The Road Not Taken

Two roads diverged in a yellow wood,
And sorry I could not travel both
And be one traveler, long I stood
And looked down one as far as I could
To where it bent in the undergrowth;

Then took the other, as just as fair,
And having perhaps the better claim,
Because it was grassy and wanted wear;
Though as for that, the passing there
Had worn them really about the same,

And both that morning equally lay
In leaves no step had trodden black.
Oh, I kept the first for another day!
Yet knowing how way leads on to way,
I doubted if I should ever come back.

I shall be telling this with a sigh
Somewhere ages and ages hence:
Two roads diverged in a wood, and I—
I took the one less traveled by,
And that has made all the difference.

—Robert Frost

LESSON 17

/ɑ/ as in father
/ɔ/ as in law
(*Dictionary marks:* ȧ, ȯ)

To make the /ɑ/ sound, your mouth should be well open and your lips should be relaxed. Keep the sound short.

Notice that the sound /ɔ/, as in the word "law," is made with your lips forming a vertical oval.

Remember that /ɑ/ and /ɔ/ are vowels, and that all vowels are voiced.

I. /ɑ/ Words

Listen to your instructor pronounce these words. Repeat them aloud in class and practice them afterward.

1. arch	9. bar	17. far	25. marble
2. are	10. bark	18. farm	26. mark
3. arm	11. barn	19. farther	27. modern
4. art	12. bother	20. father	28. park
5. obstacle	13. calm	21. garden	29. part
6. obstinate	14. card	22. hard	30. shark
7. omnipotent	15. column	23. heart	31. star
8. opera	16. dark	24. large	32. tardy

II. /ɑ/ Words and Sentences

Your instructor will pronounce the following pairs of words and the sentences for you to repeat aloud in class and practice when you are alone.

1. obstinate, argue
   The obstinate man liked to argue with others.
2. arm
   The football player broke his arm in yesterday's game.
3. car, dark
   The car overturned on the steep, dark curve.
4. bother, father
   He didn't bother to discuss the matter with his father.
5. heart
   His heart was pounding when he finished the race.

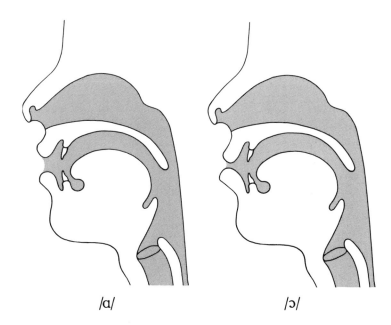

/ɑ/   /ɔ/

III. /ɔ/ Words

1. almost	10. ball	19. talk	28. draw
2. already	11. caught	20. tall	29. jaw
3. also	12. cause	21. taught	30. law
4. always	13. fall	22. thought	31. raw
5. auction	14. fought	23. trawl	32. saw
6. automatic	15. hall	24. vault	
7. autumn	16. quarter	25. walk	
8. awkward	17. salt	26. war	
9. ought	18. sawed	27. wardrobe	

IV. /ɔ/ Words and Sentences

The following words and sentences provide additional practice for you on one of the sounds of this lesson.

1. lawyer, thought
   Has the lawyer given the problem much thought?
2. almost, drawing
   He almost completed his drawing.
3. law, autumn
   The turnpike law is being revised this autumn.
4. also, saw
   They also saw their old classmates.
5. ought, quarter
   She ought to leave a quarter tip.

V. Contrasting Pairs

/ɑ/ – /ɔ/

1. barn – born	4. park – pork
2. card – cord	5. part – port
3. farce – force	

THE SOUNDS OF AMERICAN ENGLISH

VI. Poetry

Listen as your instructor reads this poem aloud. Follow along and underline each occurrence of the /ɑ/ and /ɔ/ sounds. You may have an opportunity to read a portion of the poem in class; practice this reading by yourself as well.

Girl's-Eye View of Relatives: First Lesson

The thing to remember about fathers is, they're men.
A girl has to keep it in mind.
They are dragon-seekers, bent on improbable rescues.
Scratch any father, you find
Someone chock-full of qualms and romantic terrors,
Believing change is a threat—
Like your first shoes with heels on, like your first bicycle
It took such months to get.

Walk in strange woods, they warn you about the snakes there.
Climb, and they fear you'll fall.
Books, angular boys, or swimming in deep water—
Fathers mistrust them all.
Men are the worriers. It is difficult for them
To learn what they must learn:
How you have a journey to take and very likely,
For a while, will not return.

—Phyllis McGinley

LESSON 18

/ʃ/, /ʒ/ as in *she* and *azure*
(*Dictionary marks:* sh, zh)

Both of these consonants are formed by making an air funnel of your mouth and lips. The tip of the tongue is close to the gum ridge just behind the upper teeth, the middle of the tongue is close to the roof of the mouth, and the sides of the tongue are against the back teeth. The lips are pushed outward, the upper and lower front teeth are brought almost together, and the air comes over the tongue and through the lips.

/ʃ/ is pronounced just as /ʒ/, except that /ʒ/ is voiced. Put your hand securely against your larynx; then begin to say /ʃ/, prolong it, and change to /ʒ/ without stopping, in order to feel its slight vibration as you produce the voiced sound.

I. /ʃ/ and /ʒ/ Words

Listen to your instructor pronounce these words. Repeat them aloud in class and practice them afterward.

/ʃ/	/ʒ/
1. share	1. azure
2. sugar	2. casual
3. machine	3. division

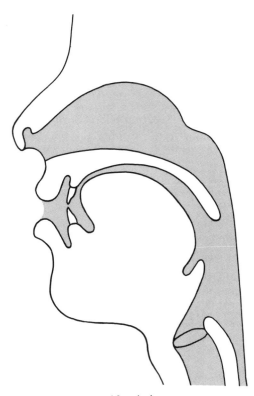

/ʃ/, /ʒ/

4. mission	4. fusion
5. nation	5. measure
6. ocean	6. occasion
7. pension	7. Persian
8. tissue	8. seizure
9. vicious	9. usual
10. fish	10. vision
11. wash	11. beige
12. wish	12. corsage

II. Contrasting Pairs

Your instructor will pronounce the following pairs of words and sentences for you to repeat aloud in class and practice when you are alone. Note that the meaning in the first three pairs below depends on the distinction between /ʃ/ and /ʒ/.

1. Aleutian – allusion
   They headed for the Aleutian Islands.
   They made an allusion to my idea.
2. dilution – delusion
   We didn't want a dilution!
   What a delusion!
3. glacier – glazier
   Did they cross the glacier?
   Did they call the glazier?
4. position – precision
   Verify the position!
   We want precision.
5. rush – rouge
   Please don't rush.
   Hand me the rouge.

III. /ʃ/ and /ʒ/ Words Often Mispronounced

Listen to your instructor pronounce these words. Repeat them aloud in class and practice them afterward.

/ʃ/

1. Charlotte
2. Chicago
3. shrank
4. shred
5. shrill
6. shrimp
7. shrub
8. shrug
9. fission
10. fissure
11. luxury
12. mention
13. Michigan

/ʒ/

1. anesthesia
2. Asiatic
3. leisure
4. pleasure
5. treasure
6. barrage
7. camouflage
8. cortege
9. garage
10. loge
11. massage
12. mirage
13. prestige
14. rouge
15. sabotage

IV. /ʃ/ and /ʒ/ Words and Sentences

The following words and sentences provide additional practice for you on the sounds of this lesson.

1. gara*g*e : /ʒ/
   Will you please take the garbage to the garage?
2. *sh*rimp : /ʃ/
   Would you care for shrimp?
3. plea*s*ure : /ʒ/
   With pleasure we pledged our support.
4. bei*g*e : /ʒ/
   Do you see the girl with a badge pinned on a beige dress?
5. men*ti*on, lu*x*ury : /ʃ/, /ʃ/
   We needn't mention how we enjoyed such luxury.
6. *sh*rink : /ʃ/
   Will those sox shrink in hot water?
7. presti*g*e : /ʒ/
   The award gave him prestige.
8. *Ch*arlotte, Mi*ch*igan : /ʃ/, /ʃ/
   Charlotte from Michigan will be our next speaker.

V. Poetry

Listen as your instructor reads this poem aloud. Follow along and underline each occurrence of the /ʃ/ and /ʒ/ sounds. You may have an opportunity to read a portion of the poem in class; practice this reading by yourself as well.

From *Kubla Khan*

In Xanadu did Kubla Khan
A stately pleasure-dome decree:
Where Alph, the sacred river, ran
Through caverns measureless to man
     Down to a sunless sea.
So twice five miles of fertile ground
With walls and towers were girdled round:
And there were gardens bright with sinuous rills,
Where blossomed many an incense-bearing tree;
And here were forests ancient as the hills,
Enfolding sunny spots of greenery.

But oh! that deep romantic chasm which slanted
Down the green hill athwart a cedarn cover!
A savage place! as holy and enchanted
As e'er beneath a waning moon was haunted
By woman wailing for her demon-lover!
And from this chasm, with ceaseless turmoil seething,
As if this earth in fast thick pants were breathing,
A mighty fountain momently was forced:
Amid whose swift half-intermitted burst
Huge fragments vaulted like rebounding hail,
Or chaffy grain beneath the thresher's flail:
And 'mid these dancing rocks at once and ever
It flung up momently the sacred river.
Five miles meandering with a mazy motion
Through wood and dale the sacred river ran,

Then reached the caverns measureless to man,
And sank in tumult to a lifeless ocean:
And 'mid this tumult Kubla heard from far
Ancestral voices prophesying war!
    The shadow of the dome of pleasure
    Floated midway on the waves;
    Where was heard the mingled measure
    From the fountain and the caves.
It was a miracle of rare device,
A sunny pleasure-dome with caves of ice!

               —Samuel Taylor Coleridge

LESSON 19

/tʃ/, /dʒ/ as in *chair* and *just*
(*Dictionary marks:* ch, j)

In the pronunciation of these consonants the tip of the tongue first presses against the upper gum ridge to stop the air stream. Next, the tongue suddenly releases the air pressure, changing rapidly from the /t/ position through the /ʃ/ position to complete /tʃ/, or changing rapidly from the /d/ position through the /ʒ/ position to complete /dʒ/. The lips are slightly protruded and the upper and lower teeth are brought almost together.

/tʃ/ is pronounced by the same positions as /dʒ/, except that /dʒ/ is voiced.

I. /tʃ/ and /dʒ/ Words Often Mispronounced

Listen to your instructor pronounce these words. Repeat them aloud in class and practice them afterward.

/tʃ/	/dʒ/
1. cello	1. genuine
2. aperture	2. gesture
3. barbiturate	3. giblet
4. congratulate	4. judicial
5. pasture	5. judicious
6. picture	6. adjective

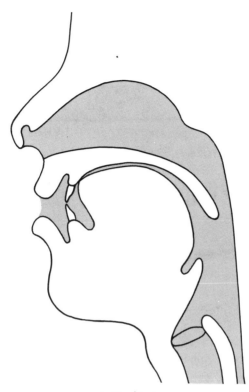

/tʃ/, /dʒ/

7. posthumous
8. virtuous
9. catch
10. niche

7. agile
8. education
9. largess
10. longevity

II. Voicing Exercises for /dʒ/

You may be pronouncing the /tʃ/ sound correctly, but are you fully voicing the /dʒ/ sound? A common error in all speech regions of the United States is the substitution of /tʃ/ for /dʒ/, especially in the middle and at the end of the words.

	/tʃ/	/dʒ/
1.	etch	– edge
2.	etches	– edges
3.	march	– Marge
4.	matches	– Madge's
5.	rich	– ridge

/dʒ/ words

1. agent		6.	age
2. engine		7.	cabbage
3. imagine		8.	huge
4. logic		9.	language
5. soldier		10.	orange

III. Contrasting Pairs

Your instructor will pronounce the following pairs of words and the sentences for you to repeat aloud in class and practice when you are alone.

1. ashes – actual : /ʃ/ – /tʃ/
   Those old ashes are part of the actual remains.
2. question – session : /tʃ/ – /ʃ/
   It's time for the question and answer session.
3. seeds – siege : /dz/ – /dʒ/
   The seeds were planted for the great siege.
4. aged – Asia : /dʒ/ – /ʒ/
   The aged man immigrated from Central Asia.
5. heads – hedge : /dz/ – /dʒ/
   Don't cut off the flower heads on our front hedge.
6. mashes – matches : /ʃ/ – /tʃ/
   He always mashes an old box of matches.
7. mush – much : /ʃ/ – /tʃ/
   If it's mush, she won't eat much.
8. measure – major : /ʒ/ – /dʒ/
   This measure is necessary for major repairs.

IV. /tʃ/ and /dʒ/ Words and Sentences

The following words and sentences provide additional practice for you on the sounds of this lesson.

1. *ch*eese : /tʃ/
   Some people like cheese and crackers for dessert.
2. kit*ch*en : /tʃ/
   Everything in the kitchen was made of stainless steel.
3. mer*ch*ant : /tʃ/
   The merchant seaman traveled all over the world.
4. ea*ch* : /tʃ/
   There was a present for each of us.
5. *j*ump : /dʒ/
   The sound of the horn made her jump.
6. mana*g*er : /dʒ/
   Please let me talk to the store manager.
7. *ju*d*ge* : (both) /dʒ/
   Were you able to judge who was right?
8. langua*g*e : /dʒ/
   I like the speaker's use of language.

V. Prose

Listen as your instructor reads this selection aloud. Follow along and note that all occurrences of the /tʃ/ and /dʒ/ sounds are emphasized. You may have the opportunity to read a portion of the letter in class; practice this reading by yourself as well.

To the Countess of ____

Dear Lady * *,

Your recollection and invitation do me great honour; but I am going to be "married, and can't come." My intended is two hundred miles off, and the moment my business here is arranged,

I must set out in a great hurry to be happy. Miss Milbanke is the good-natured person who has undertaken me, and, of course, I am very much in love, and as silly as all single gentlemen must be in that sentimental situation. I have been accepted these three weeks; but when the event will take place, I don't exactly know. It depends partly upon lawyers, who are never in a hurry. One can be sure of nothing; but, at present, there appears no other interruption to this intention, which seems as mutual as possible, and now no secret, though I did not tell first—and all our relatives are congratulating away to right and left in the most fatiguing manner.

You perhaps know the lady. She is niece to Lady Melbourne, and cousin to Lady Cowper and others of your acquaintance, and has no fault, except being a great deal too good for me, and that I must pardon, if nobody else should. It might have been *two* years ago, and, if it had, would have saved me a world of trouble. She has employed the interval in refusing about half a dozen of my particular friends (as she did me once, by the way) and has taken me at last, for which I am very much obliged to her. I wish it was well over, for I do hate bustle, and there is no marrying without some; and then, I must not marry in a black coat, they tell me, and I can't bear a blue one.

Pray forgive me for scribbling all this nonsense. You know I must be serious all the rest of my life, and this is a parting piece of buffoonery, which I write with tears in my eyes, expecting to be agitated. Believe me, most seriously and sincerely your obliged servant,

Byron.

LESSON 20

/h/ as in *h*ad
/j/ as in *y*ear
(*Dictionary marks:* h, y)

The sound which you should have the least difficulty in producing is the sound of the letter *h*. This sound, which is /h/, is simply an exhalation of air. The vowel that follows it modifies or changes the sound of /h/ to conform to the vowel sound.

I. /h/ Words and Sentences

Your instructor will pronounce the following words and the sentences for you to repeat aloud in class and practice when you are alone.

1. he, half, hurry
   He read half of the week's assignment in a hurry.
2. happy, lighthouse, horizon
   We were happy to see the lighthouse on the horizon.
3. his, hello
   His cheerful "Hello" made everyone feel better.
4. Hugh, home, holidays
   Hugh was away from home during the holidays.
5. who
   Who is the main speaker today?

6. whole, hero, hear
   The whole town wanted to hear the hero.
7. ahead
   We saw some friends ahead of us.
8. behind, her, homework
   She was getting behind in her homework.
9. perhaps, rehearse, anyhow
   Perhaps we should rehearse anyhow.
10. have, height, hearth
    The architects have noted the height of the fireplace and the length of the hearth.

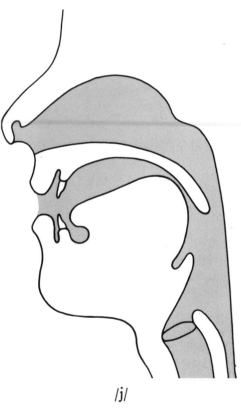

/j/

II. Words with the /h̩/ Sound

Listen to your instructor pronounce these words. Repeat them aloud in class and practice them afterward.

1. Hubert	7. humanity	12. humility
2. hue (hew, Hugh)	8. humid	13. humor
3. huge	9. humidity	14. humorist
4. Hugo	10. humiliate	15. humorous
5. human	11. humiliation	16. humus
6. humane		

The second sound of this lesson is /j/, a voiced sound in which the front of the tongue glides from a forward position in the mouth, resembling the /i/ sound, to a position in which it almost touches the roof of the mouth. The tongue then moves smoothly but rapidly into the position of the vowel following /j/. You may find it helpful to think of this sound as usually made by the letter y as in "yard," "year," and "yellow."

III. /j/ Words

Listen to your instructor pronounce these words. Repeat them aloud in class and practice them afterward.

1. usurp	11. amuse	21. onion
2. yard	12. argue	22. regulate
3. year	13. bullion	23. regular
4. yellow	14. calculate	24. reputation
5. yesterday	15. Daniel	25. spaniel
6. you (ewe, yew)	16. familiar	26. strangulate
7. young	17. figure	27. value
8. abuse	18. formulate	28. volume
9. accumulate	19. genial	
10. accurate	20. million	

IV. Words which may be pronounced correctly either with or without the /j/ sound

1. assume
2. constitute
3. due (do, dew)
4. endure
5. institute
6. knew (new, gnu)
7. newspaper
8. nuisance
9. numerous
10. resume
11. student
12. tube
13. Tuesday
14. tulip
15. tune
16. tunic

V. Contrasting Pairs

The /ju/ sound, pronounced "you," may be treated by some experts in phonetics as a separate diphthong. These practice materials may help to clarify the use of /ju/.

/u/ - /ju/

1. boot – butte
2. booty– beauty
3. coo   – cue
4. food – feud
5. moot – mute

In the next contrast drill in sentence form, note that the /j/ sound is italicized.

1. fe*u*d – food
   The feud developed over the food.
2. fool – f*u*el
   What fool forgot the fuel?
3. geni*u*s – genus
   He was a genius to classify it in that genus.

4. moot – mute
   It's a moot point if he remains mute.
5. awl – yawl
   We need an awl to repair the sails of the yawl.
6. cannon – canyon
   There's an old cannon in the canyon.

VI. Poetry

The following familiar poem by Lewis Carroll is filled with /j/ sounds.   While your instructor reads the poem aloud, follow along and underline each occurrence.   You may have an opportunity to read a portion of the poem in class; practice this reading by yourself as well.

Father William

"You are old, Father William," the young man said,
   "And your hair has become very white;
And yet you incessantly stand on your head—
   Do you think, at your age, it is right?"

"In my youth," Father William replied to his son,
   "I feared it might injure the brain;
But, now that I'm perfectly sure I have none,
   Why, I do it again and again."

"You are old," said the youth, "as I mentioned before,
   And have grown most uncommonly fat;
Yet you turned a back-somersault in at the door—
   Pray, what is the reason of that?"

"In my youth," said the sage, as he shook his gray locks,
   "I kept all my limbs very supple
By the use of this ointment—one shilling the box—
   Allow me to sell you a couple?"

"You are old," said the youth, "and your jaws are too weak
   For anything tougher than suet;
Yet you finished the goose, with the bones and the beak—
   Pray, how did you manage to do it?"

"In my youth," said his father, "I took to the law,
   And argued each case with my wife;
And the muscular strength which it gave to my jaw,
   Has lasted the rest of my life."

"You are old," said the youth, "one would hardly suppose
   That your eye was as steady as ever;
Yet you balanced an eel on the end of your nose—
   What made you so awfully clever?"

"I have answered three questions and that is enough,"
   Said his father; "don't give yourself airs!
Do you think I can listen all day to such stuff?
   Be off, or I'll kick you downstairs!"

—Lewis Carroll